Greatest Moments in Virginia Tech Football History

Edited by
FRANCIS J. FITZGERALD

AN EPIC SPORTS BOOK

The Hokies' Biggest Games, Coaches & Players

DEDICATION

To Jerry Claiborne, who made Virginia Tech a winner, and to the late Frank Loria, who set the example for all future Hokies.

Research assistance: Dave Smith and the Virginia Tech Sports Information Office, Virginia Tech Special Collections, Chris Colston, Dave Krachel and Bob Roller.

ISBN 1-928846-44-0

COVER AND BOOK DESIGN: Lisa Eads, Photographics, Birmingham, Ala.
PHOTO IMAGING: Photographics, Birmingham, Ala.
PUBLISHED BY: Epic Sports, Birmingham, Ala.

DEDICATION DAY MILE'S STADIUM V.P.I. BLACK

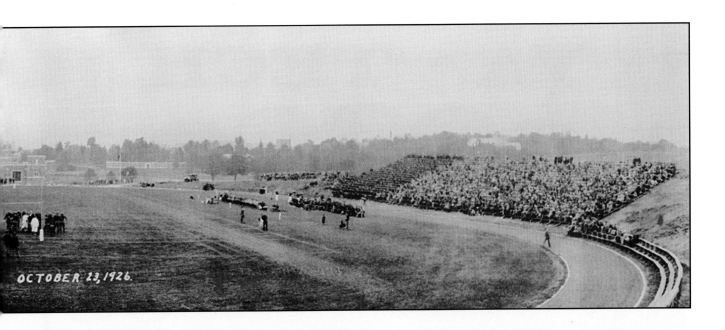

OCTOBER 23, 1926.

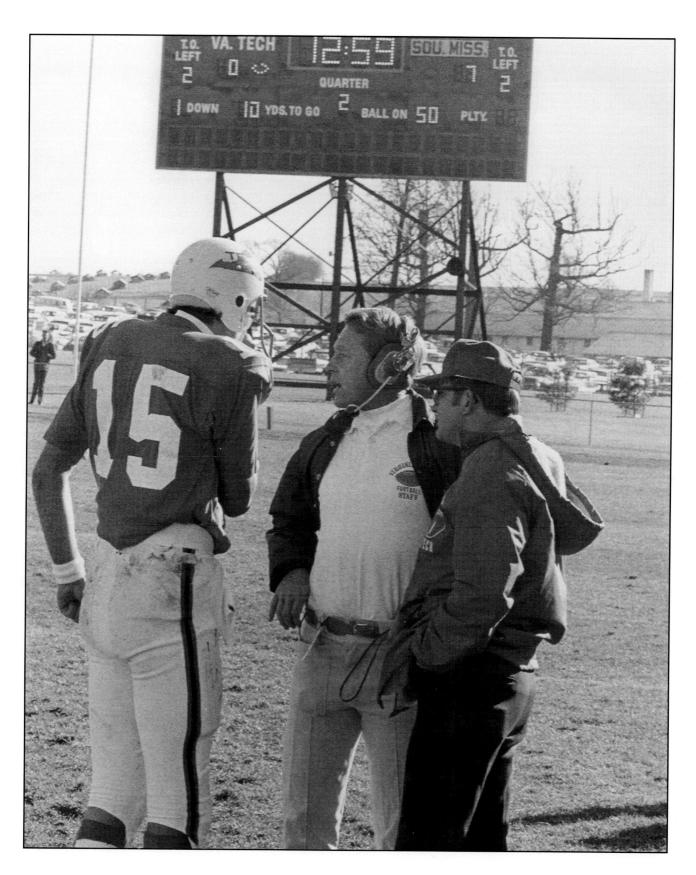

STANDING—Left to Right: Noenstine, Kasun, Hall, Murphy, Jennings, Simmons, Cunningham, Dillon, Huffman, H. Howard, Noblitzell, Copenhaver, Netts, Porterfield, Nite, Grieus, Captain (Insert); Seaman, Negri, Yorke, Oliver, F. Howard, Palmer, Miles, Anderson, Waldrup, Neale, Beamon, Goddie, Francis, Holsclaw.

KNEELING—Left to Right: Morgan, Retnick, Robinson, Casey, Clark, Spruill, English, MacIntire, Smeak, Maddox, Manager; Stark, Assistant Coach; Notchkiss, Assistant Coach; Younger, Assistant Coach; Redd, Head Coach; "Skibo" Maynard, Mascot; Tilson, Assistant Coach; Thomas, G. Smith, Ochs, Mills, Ottaway, Tyler, W. Smith, Woodard, Day.

V. P. I. vs. University of Kentucky at Blacksburg, Va.

Game Called at 2:30 P. M.   **OCTOBER 22, 1932**   Admission $2.00 plus tax

Write C. P. MILES, Director of Athletics, Virginia Polytechnic Institute, Blacksburg, Virginia, for Reservations

16

Table of Contents

Carpenter, Virginia Tech Roll Over Middies

ANNAPOLIS, Md., Nov. 21, 1903 — Hunter Carpenter led Virginia Tech to its greatest victory in 14 years of playing football by defeating Navy, 11-0.

Carpenter, the right half for VPI, scored a touchdown in the first four minutes of the game on a 50-yard run and booted the point-after kick to give the visitors a 7-0 lead.

Late in the second half, Carpenter added a 46-yard field goal to boost VPI's lead to 11-0.

Virginia Tech	7	4	–	11
Navy	0	0	–	0

A week earlier, Washington & Jefferson's William DeWitt kicked a 42-yard field goal against Navy in their 16-0 win.

Along with Carpenter, Clarence Byrd, John Counselman and George Willson stood out for VPI against the Midshipmen.

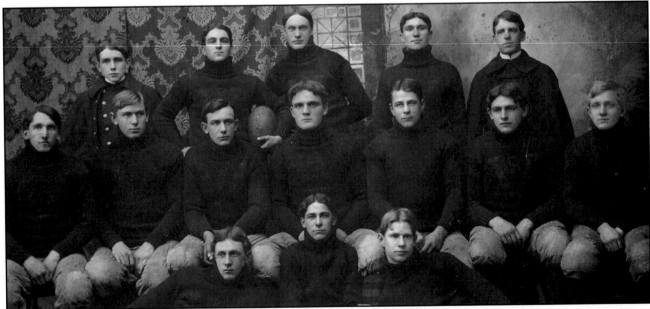

• *The 1903 Tech squad, who were coached by C.A. Lueder, posted a record of 5-1.*

Hunter Carpenter: He Bled Maroon and Wanted to Beat Virginia

Virginia Tech's greatest football player from its early days wanted to beat the University of Virginia so bad that he transferred to another school to do so.

Hunter Carpenter put Tech on the football map with its wins over Navy in 1903 and Army in 1905. But the opponent that he wanted to beat the most was the cross-state school in Charlottesville.

Tech had played Virginia eight times from 1895 through 1904 and had lost in all eight meetings.

Carpenter, however, had transferred to the University of North Carolina that fall and was a starter on the Tar Heels squad. It was written in the local newspapers that Carpenter had transferred to UNC and was playing on the football team.

What newspaper writers didn't know was that this was Carpenter's seventh year in college. A native of Clifton Forge, Va., he had enrolled at Tech in 1898, when he was only 15. At 128 pounds, his goal was to make the football team and beat UVa — one of the better Eastern teams at the time.

Carpenter would eventually join the Tech football squad in 1900, at age 17 — but under the alias of Walter Brown. Carpenter's father had forbid him from taking up the game because of his size. So Carpenter used the fake name to protect his identity.

He would eventually survive the 1900 season and would play the next one under his own name.

In 1902, Carpenter was named team captain.

In 1904, Carpenter lost to the Wahoos again, but he would be playing for the Tar Heels.

The Gobblers would have its best season in 1905, posting a 9-1 record, and Carpenter was its star.

Prior to the 1905 Virginia game, the Wahoos almost cancelled the game, claiming that Carpenter had been playing professionally. Virginia even asked that Carpenter sign an affidavit stating that he hadn't been tom play for pay. Carpenter denied the charges and offered to not play that afternoon.

Finally, after a 30-minute stalemate, the Wahoos backed down and went on with the game. Tech won, 11-0, and got that their first ever win over their rival.

But in the game's final three minutes a fight broke out when Carpenter slugged a Virginia lineman.

Carpenter was later ejected.

Following the game, Tech wrote *The Roanoke Times* a letter stating: "The recent charges of professionalism made by the management of the University of Virginia team and spread broadcast throughout the country is a mere popy (sic) cock story created to win popular sympathy for the University ... ."

After the letter was published, Virginia opted to not play the Gobblers in 1906 — and the series didn't renew until 1923.

Carpenter didn't return to the Tech team in 1906. He went on to graduate from Tech in civil engineering and became a contractor.

He was elected to the College Football Hall of Fame in 1953.

Carpenter's 2 TD's Force Army to Surrender

WEST POINT, N.Y., Oct. 14, 1905 — Hunter Carpenter scored twice this afternoon against the Cadets to give VPI a 16-6 victory.

The Gobblers scored first. Carpenter ran 25 yards around end to set up a field goal. Carpenter booted the kick to put VPI ahead, 4-0.

Five minutes later, Carpenter romped outside left end for another 25 yards to set up VPI's second score. Harry Treadwell then took the ball over for the touchdown to give VPI a 10-0 lead.

The Virginians scored once more in the first half, with George Willson carrying for the touchdown. VPI led, 16-0, at halftime.

Army opened the second half with a drive that gave the Cadets their only score. Bill Christy ripped the middle of the VPI line for the touchdown to narrow the score to 16-6.

The remainder of the game was spent with both teams' defenses aggressively closing down the other team's attack.

• *Hunter Carpenter scored 2 touchdowns against Army.*

Virginia Tech	16	0	—	16
Army	0	6	—	6

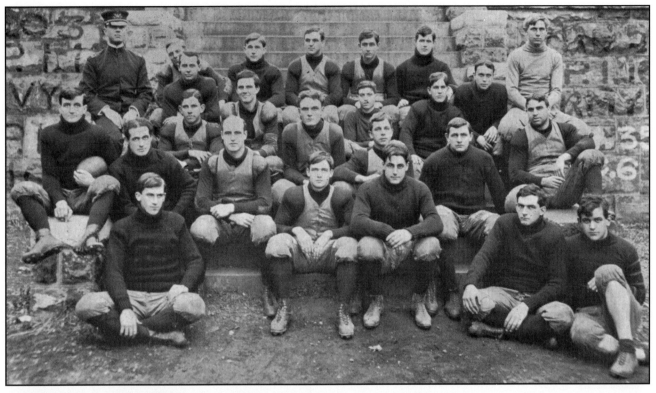

• *C.P. Miles' 1905 Gobblers put together an impressive 9-1 record.*

Peake Leads VPI Past Powerhouse Colgate

HAMILTON, N.Y., Oct. 8, 1927 — For the first time in twenty seasons, Colgate was defeated on its home field. Virginia Polytechnic Institute, who had traveled a long way to meet the Maroon, came away with a 6-0 victory this afternoon.

VPI's light, but fast backfield was unable to get outside Colgate's ends in the early portion of the contest, so the Gobblers began to mix in an aerial attack.

Late in the first quarter, a 10-yard pass and a 20-yard run by Frank Peake put the ball inside Colgate's 15-yard line. The Colgate defense managed to put the brakes on VPI's advance and a field goal attempt was short.

In the second quarter VPI got the ball on its 30-yard line and after a series of passes and end runs by Mitchell Mattox and Peake moved the ball to the Colgate 10.

Two plunges by Peake covered the remaining distance for the touchdown. The point-after kick was wide.

The Maroon tried to rally in the final quarter but threatened only once, when Thomas Dowler, a substitute, returned a punt back to the VPI 45 and later caught a pass from George Brewer at the VPI 20-yard line. Brewer was intercepted on the next play and Colgate never got close again.

• *Gobblers head coach Andy Gustafson.*

Virginia Tech	0	6	0	0	—	6
Colgate	0	0	0	0	—	0

• *Top: Frank Peake (right) ran for nearly 200 yards and the game's only TD. Below: Andy Gustafson's Gobblers put together a 5-4 record in 1927.*

Tech's Triumph Over Georgia Stuns South

ATHENS, Ga., Oct. 1, 1932 — Virginia Tech's 7-6 surprise win over Georgia today has left Southern football fans groggy.

It was known that Georgia was not up to its 1931 strength, but there were few who conceded the Blacksburg Gobblers much of a chance against a team that had beaten them, 40-0, a year ago.

Tech outfought and out-maneuvered a youthful Georgia squad for three quarters, then the fiesty Bulldogs put together a last-minute march for a touchdown that left a crowd of 7,000 filled with hope for the rest of the season.

After a talk by Bill Younger, the Gobblers' assistant coach, who had been turning out good teams at Davidson College in North Carolina for more than a decade, Tech was able to capitalize on their hard-plunging offensive attack.

Throughout the first quarter, the Gobblers kept the ball in Georgia's territory. Then in the second period, the break came that Tech had been long working for.

Al Casey, a fleet back who was substituting for Charlie Morgan, caught a 47-yard kick from Georgia's Willy Sullivan and ran it back to the Georgia 35.

Ray Mills unleashed a 31-yard pass to Casey that moved the ball down to the Georgia 4. Mills and Casey then pounded the Bulldog line to put the ball at the Georgia six-inch line.

Casey soared over the Bulldogs' line for the touchdown. Gene Hite booted the extra point to give Tech a 7-0 lead.

In the third quarter, Georgia began to gather strength and marched to the Tech 6 before being stopped by the Gobbler defense.

With five minutes left in the fourth quarter and the ball at their 15 Georgia mounted a final drive toward the Tech end zone.

A 7-yard run by Homer Key and two passes from Sullivan to Key and Sam Brown put the ball at midfield.

Brown ripped for five yards, Bill David added 6, and Brown ran off-tackle for 10 to move the ball to the Tech 29.

Following a 5-yard penalty against Tech, David crashed over the middle for 22 yards to put the ball at the Tech 2.

After two attempts, David rammed over for the touchdown. Paul Hart's dropkick for the extra point was blocked by Tech captain Bill Grinus.

Virginia Tech	0	7	0	0	—	7
Georgia	0	0	0	6	—	6

• *Top: Gobblers halfback Duncan Holsclaw sweeps around right end against Georgia. Below: Virginia Tech roared to an 8-1 record in 1932.*

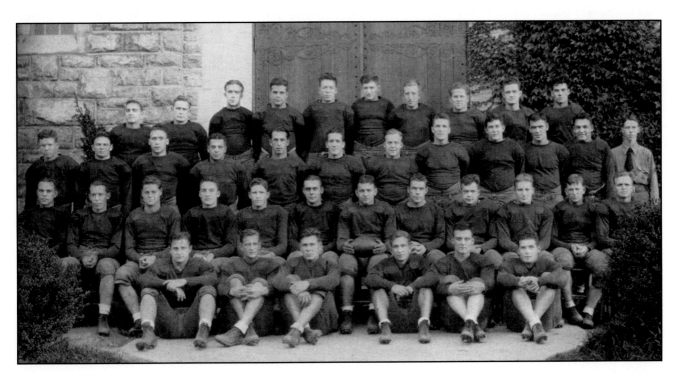

McClure Boots Gobblers Over Georgetown

BLACKSBURG, Oct. 4, 1941 — Roger McClure, the 190 lb. junior guard who handles the kicking duties for the Gobblers, kicked Georgetown out of the national spotlight with a 19-yard third-quarter kick that gave Tech its biggest win since defeating Georgia in 1932.

McClure's kick followed the recovery of Georgetown's Frank Dornfield's fumble on the Hoyas' 26 by Bob Smith, a Gobbler halfback, who was the spark of a football upset that excited 7,000 Tech Homecoming fans and will be talked about by football coaches and sportswriters for weeks to come.

Smith ripped to the Georgetown 15, then Jack Gallagher gave Tech fans a scare when he fumbled the ball for a 9-yard loss.

Gallagher bounced back with a pass to fullback Mason Blandford at the Georgetown 16, then tossed one to end Gerald Clark at the 9.

On fourth down and four yards still needed for a first down, Tech coach Jimmy Kitts looked toward his bench and motioned for McClure to enter the game.

With Gene Wheeler holding, McClure booted the ball through the goalposts and ended Georgetown's hopes for a scoreless tie.

Last year in Washington, Georgetown — who was the No. 1-ranked team in several polls — trampled Tech, 46-4.

The Hoyas got an opportunity to get on the scoreboard in the game's final seven minutes when Benny Reiges recovered a Tech fumble at the Gobblers' 16.

The Hoyas' attack sputtered when Reiges fumbled and center Ed Derringer grabbed it at the 16. Three incomplete passes ended Georgetown's scoring chances.

Both squads muffed scoring chances in the first half of the game.

Tech knocked on the door first when Wheeler intercepted Hoya quarterback Benny Bulvin's pass at the Georgetown 35 and returned it to the 23.

Gallagher ran over right tackle for six yards to move the ball to the 17.

Trouble came calling for Tech on the next play when Louis Falcone intercepted Gallagher's pass at the 8 to end Tech's drive.

In the second quarter, Georgetown got its chance. Dornfield aimed downfield for John Doolan over the middle for a 35-yard strike that moved the Hoyas to the Tech 23. Doolan circled left end for 9 yards to reach the Tech 14.

Finally, the Gobblers dug in and stopped Bulvin and Doolan, taking over at the Tech 16.

When the contest was over, 2,100 cadets spilled out onto the field and hoisted their heroes on their shoulders.

Georgetown	0	0	0	0	—	0
Virginia Tech	0	0	3	0	—	3

• *Top: The Gobblers' 3-0 win over Georgetown, who was No. 1 for most of 1940, made headlines across the country the next day. Below: Jimmy Kitts' 1941 Tech squad went 6-4.*

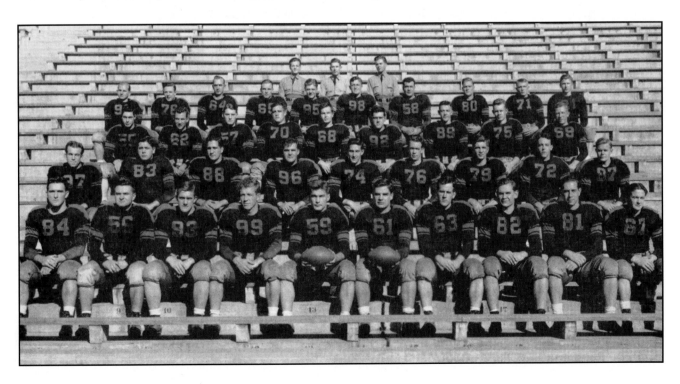

Cincinnati's 2 Third-Quarter TD's Tame Gobblers

EL PASO, Tex., Jan. 1, 1947 — Playing in weather that hockey players are more used to, the Cincinnati Bearcats put together a hard-charging ground attack, sparked by halfback Roger Stephen, which battered Virginia Tech, 18-6, this afternoon in the 12th Sun Bowl.

For two quarters, the game was a scoreless battle between two massive lines.

Late in the first quarter, Tech drove to the Cincinnati 2-yard line. But after four attempts, the Bearcats held Tech at the 2. It was a problem the Gobblers had faced several times this season.

Cincinnati needed a half to get going, but once their motor was heated up, the Bearcats exploded for a pair of quick third-quarter touchdowns and added another in the game's final three minutes.

Cincinnati fielded the second-half kickoff and raced 75 yards to their first score. It took the Bearcats three minutes 20 seconds to post the first TD. The second 15-yard penalty nullified a Bearcats' touchdown, but they scored moments later.

Stephens got the Bearcats going with a 26-yard run to the Tech 49 on the first play of the second half. Stephens and Al Sabato each gained 11 yards to move the ball to the Tech 27.

Don McMillan passed to Elbert Nickel, who lateraled to Stephens at the Tech 11 and the Bearcat halfback ran into the Tech end zone untouched.

But it was called back on a clipping penalty.

Starting at the Tech 26, Hal Johnson and Sabato combined on carries to put the ball at the 14. Johnson then ripped up the middle for the needed 14 yards for the touchdown and a 6-0 lead. John Sarsfield missed the extra-point kick as well as the next two attempts.

Later in the third quarter, Stephens led the Bearcats from their 37 to another touchdown in seven plays. Sabato scored on a 2-yard dive over the middle to give Cincinnati a 12-0 lead.

At the beginning of the fourth quarter, the Gobblers got a break when a 15-yard unnecessary roughness penalty Tech the ball at the Cincinnati 21.

Beasley quickly picked up 10 yards on a run off right tackle. A penalty against the Bearcats put the ball at the 6. Beasley scored three plays later on a 2-yard run to narrow the score to 12-6. Ross Orr missed the extra-point kick.

Cincinnati turned an interception into a touchdown in the final three minutes of the contest.

After Tech had moved the ball to midfield, Johnson snatched Beard's pass, returning it to the Tech 20. At that point, Johnson lateraled to Bill Smyth who was quickly tackled. Four carries put the ball at the Tech 2. McMillan scored on a quarterback sneak to seal the 18-6 win for the Bearcats.

Virginia Tech	0	0	0	6	—	6
Cincinnati	0	0	12	6	—	18

• *Top: The 1946 Tech offense. Below: The Gobblers traveled to El Paso with a 3-4-2 record.*

Gobblers Turn Up the Heat in Win Over Clemson

CLEMSON, S.C., Oct. 2, 1954 — With the temperature at 95 degrees, Virginia Tech made it hotter for the Tigers by converting a trio of Clemson mistakes into Tech touchdowns.

The 18-7 win was the Gobblers' biggest in a season of smashing triumphs and most noted since their 1941 defeat of Georgetown.

Wonder Boys Howie Wright and Dickie Beard led Tech's assault.

The Gobblers turned three Clemson mistakes — a pass interception and two fumbles — into a pair of touchdowns and a 12-0 lead in the first nine minutes of the opening quarter.

Tech scored again late in the second quarter to take an 18-0 lead at halftime.

Clemson only crossed into Tech's territory twice, but managed to spend most of the second half in the Gobblers' backyard.

Beard scored first for Tech with a 14-yard run. Quarterback Johnny Dean scored the next two TD's as the Gobblers posted 129 yards rushing and 31 through the air in the first half.

Overall, Clemson had more impressive stats: 154 on the ground and 153 in the air. Tech finished with 183 yards rushing and 43 passing. Wright and Beard combined for 150 yards rushing.

A pass interception by Dean on the game's second play gave Tech the ball at the Clemson 38.

Beard scored on a 14-yard counter play to the left, twisting past the secondary, with 10:35 left in the first quarter.

Clemson fumbled two plays after the ensuing kickoff and a holding penalty pushed Tech up to the Clemson 14. Wright and Beard moved the ball to the Clemson 1. Dean then scored on a quarterback sneak.

Later in the second quarter, Tech stopped Clemson on its 31. Wright and Beard moved the ball to the Clemson 22 in five plays and a pass from Dean to Beard went to the 4. Dean ran a bootleg to the right for the touchdown.

In the third quarter, Clemson marched from its 27 to the Tech 1, but Bill Cranwell stopped Clemson's Joe Pagliei after he had taken a fourth-down pass and was downed on the one-foot line.

On the next series, Clemson drove from its 35 to the Tech 39 in six plays. Don King then connected with Harry Hicks at the Tech 5 and he ran the remaining distance for the TD, with more than 10 minutes left in the game.

Wright, a whiz kid against North Carolina State and Wake Forest, ran for 76 yards to bring his season total to 292. Beard logged 74 yards to raise his total to 201.

Virginia Tech	12	6	0	0	— 18
Clemson	0	0	0	7	— 7

• *Right: Virginia Tech's famed "Light Brigade." Below: Frank Moseley (left) and his 1954 coaching staff.*

Carroll Dale:
Big Play
End for the Hokies

Carroll Dale, a native of Wise, Va., was Virginia Tech's first all-America player, being picked by the Football Writers Association of America (*Look* magazine) and Newspaper Enterprise Association in 1959. He was named to The Associated Press' second team all-America squads in 1958 and again in 1959.

In his first game as a freshman, he played but didn't start. For the next 39 games he was a starter and led the Hokies in pass receiving all four seasons.

In 1957, *Saturday Evening Post* named Dale the best lineman in the country.

As a junior, he was named Southern Conference player of the year.

As a senior in 1959, he had 17 receptions for 408 yards and six touchdowns.

He also was awarded the Jacobs Blocking Trophy for being the Southern Conference's best lineman in 1958 and 1959.

Dale finished his career at Tech with 67 receptions for 1,195 yards and 15 touchdowns.

He later played for the Green Bay Packers on Vince Lombardi's championship seasons of 1961, '62, '65 '66 and '67, including the first two Super Bowls, and later for the Minnesota Vikings in Super Bowl VIII, and played in the Pro Bowl in 1969, '70 and '71.

He also played briefly for the Los Angles Rams.

Dale still owns the record for "best catch" average in Packers' history. His average during his eight seasons with Green Bay was 19.7 yards on 275 receptions.

Earle Edwards, who coached at North Carolina State when Dale played for Tech, best described Dale's talent: "We double-teamed him the whole game; you have to, he's a great athlete."

Dale was named to the College Football Hall of Fame in 1987.

The Dale File

	Rec.	Yards	TD's
1956	8	157	3
1957	17	171	0
1958	25	459	6
1959	17	408	6
Total	67	1,195	15

Southern Conference
Player of the Year — 1958
All-America — 1959
All-Pro — 1969, 1970, 1971

• *Carroll Dale (84) with his coach, Frank Moseley, was chosen by Saturday Evening Post as the best lineman in the country in 1957 and an all-American in 1959.*

Utz Scores Twice in Win Over Florida State

TALLAHASSEE, Fla., Oct. 26, 1963 — Opportunity knocked on Virginia Tech's door five times this afternoon and the Gobblers answered each time to grab a 31-23 win over Florida State.

Tech, who has won their last five games after a season-opening loss to Kentucky, scored four times and added a 40-yard field goal by Dickie Cranwell.

Luck turned in Tech's favor when they converted a blocked FSU punt into a touchdown and a fumble on the FSU 14 into another TD in the game's final 10 minutes.

Tech guard Newt Green broke through to block FSU punter Charlie Calhoun's kick at the Gobblers' 44. Jack Adams scooped up the ball at the FSU 38 and raced into the end zone for the TD. Cranwell booted the extra point to give Tech a 24-17 lead.

Following the kickoff, FSU quarterback Steve Tensi fumbled on the first play and Vic Kreiter made the recovery at the 14.

Tech scored in five plays, with Gobbler quarterback Bob Schweickert diving over from the FSU 1 for the touchdown. Cranwell's point-after kick gave Tech a 31-17 lead.

Tensi, the Seminoles' passing wizard, wasn't quite through. Wasting no time, he drove FSU 80 yards in 12 plays for another TD to tighten the score to 31-23. A 2-point play failed.

Tech finished up the game with 175 yards of total offense. FSU had 410. The Gobblers ran for 160 yards and 15 in the air. FSU passed for 207 and ran for 203.

FSU had to travel long distance to score its touchdowns. The Seminoles marched 86, 75 and 80 yards for its TD's. They also drove 47 yards to set up Les Murdock's 44-yard field goal.

Tech's scores came on much shorter distances due to several big breaks: a short punt to FSU's 27, an interception by Tommy Marvin, the blocked punt, Kreiter's fumble recovery and Darryl Bailey's fumble recovery that set up Cranwell's field goal.

Utz, who was Tech's workhorse all day, scored first for Tech with his 1-yard TD run. He scored his second touchdown after Marvin's interception and runback to the FSU 7. Utz swept right, stiff-armed a FSU tackler and danced into the end zone. His two TD's and Cranwell's field goal gave Tech a 17-7 lead.

Tensi tossed 10 yards to Winfred Bailey for FSU's first TD. It completed an 86-yard, 12-play drive.

A FSU field goal got the score closer at 17-10.

The Seminoles tied the score at 17-17 after a 75-yard drive in the third quarter. Dave Snyder scored on a 1-yard run. Doug Messer's extra-point kick got the score even.

| Virginia Tech | 10 | 7 | 0 | 14 | — | 31 |
| Florida State | 0 | 10 | 7 | 6 | — | 23 |

• *Top: Tech's 31-23 win over FSU was an offensive fireworks display. Below: Jerry Claiborne (middle) and his 1964 Gobblers coaching staff.*

Schweickert, Tech Upset No. 10 Florida State

BLACKSBURG, Oct. 24, 1964 — Florida State's potent passing attack of all-American quarterback Steve Tensi and all-American receiver Fred Bilentnikoff was no match for a newly-energized Tech attack led by Bob Schweickert, who led the Gobblers to a 20-11 upset of the 10th-ranked Seminoles and a 3-3 record.

The Seminoles' first loss in six games came before a Homecoming crowd of 22,000.

FSU booted a field goal the first time it got the ball but didn't get on the scoreboard again until the game's final two minutes.

The Seminoles' stars still managed to post some impressive stats. Tensi completed 21 of 39 passes for 288 yards. Bilentnikoff caught 11 of these for 182 yards — a new school season record.

Then with 2:30 left to play, Tensi drove the Seminoles 53 yards in eight plays for a touchdown. He hit Bilentnikoff for the 2-point play to wrap up the Seminoles' scoring.

Schweickert, Tech's 191 lb. senior quarterback, scored twice on 5-yard runs in the final quarter; threw a 19-yard pass on a tackle eligible play for the Gobblers' first TD in the second quarter and punted eight times for a 47.7-yard average.

His biggest kick was a 65-yarder that sailed past the FSU receivers after Tech had stopped a Seminole drive inside the 1-yard line in the final quarter.

Ken Whitely, a Tech linebacker, intercepted a Tensi pass on his 45 and returned it to the FSU 34 in the second quarter to set up Tech's first score. Eight plays later, Schweickert tossed a 19-yard pass to Erick Johnson on a tackle eligible play. Cranwell booted the extra point.

FSU had earlier driven 64 yards for a 16-yard field goal by Les Nurdock and 75 yards to the Tech 15 before Lee Narramore fumbled.

Tech led, 7-3, at halftime.

Late in the third quarter, Schweickert got Tech rolling again from its 45. He ran for 13 yards, Bobby Owens added 7, then Schweickert passed 16 yards to wingback Tommy Groom to FSU's 19. Schweickert ran around right end for 14 yards to the FSU 5.

On the next play, he ran around the other end for the touchdown. Cranwell's extra-point kick failed when the snap was bobbled.

On the second play after the ensuing kickoff, Tensi's pass was intercepted by John Raible at the FSU 35. Hugging the sideline, he was run out of bounds at the FSU 5.

Schweickert ran the last five yards for the TD, aided by a block by Utz to give Tech a 20-3 lead with 12:04 left to play.

Florida State	3	0	0	8	— 11
Virginia Tech	0	7	0	13	— 20

• *Florida State's defense piles up Gobblers halfback Sal Garcia (22) deep in their territory.*

Gobblers' Defense Holds Off FSU Aerial Assault

BLACKSBURG, Oct. 29, 1966 — Virginia Tech and Florida State gave a Lane Stadium Homecoming crowd of 31,000 and a regional television audience an autumn fireworks, display that many will remember for a long time. But in the end, it was the Tech defense that proved to be more superior and won, 23-21.

FSU's aerial bombardment and ground attack gave Tech's No. 4 nationally-ranked defense a workout. Gary Pajcic's passing and Bill Moreman's running was a fantastic show.

Tech's defense, however, made the big plays when needed.

In the first quarter, Gobblers' end Dan Mooney got the first one when he tackled FSU backup quarterback Kim Hammond in the Seminoles' end zone for a safety that put Tech up, 2-0.

Defensive back Frank Beamer was the next hero. With 1:03 left in the first half, he grabbed a Pajcic pass in the Tech end zone to halt another Seminole drive.

Following halftime, Frank Loria came up with the game's biggest play when he returned John Hosack's 54-yard punt 80 yards for a touchdown.

With the Lane Stadium crowd barely in its seats, Tech pulled off a successful on-side kick, which set up the Gobblers' final TD.

After FSU drove 86 yards in seven plays for a third-quarter touchdown, Tech's defense stopped the Seminoles' next drive inside the Tech 1-yard line.

Ken Whitley was the next Tech defender to stand tall and ensure the Gobblers' fifth win of the season. He intercepted a Pajcic pass in the fourth quarter at the Tech 15 and returned it to the 35.

Amongst all of this outstanding defense was more offense than Lane Stadium had seen in its brief history.

A total of 79 passes were thrown this afternoon. FSU was responsible for 56 of them, completing 29 for 338 yards.

Tech completed 12 of 23 attempts for 165 yards.

The two squads combined for 216 yards on the ground.

FSU finished with 449 yards of total offense; Tech had 270.

Sellers' 13 receptions equaled the record set by Fred Bilentnikoff in the 1964 Gator Bowl.

Still, Tech quarterback Tommy Stafford tossed more TD passes than the much-heralded Pajcic. Stafford had 2 scoring tosses, Pajcic had one.

Mooney's tackle of Hammond for a safety proved to be the winning difference this afternoon. An FSU delay-of-game penalty after the play nullified the kickoff that had carried to the Tech 20.

On the kickoff that followed, Tech advanced the ball from the Seminoles' 48 to to the 43. Tech was soon in the FSU end zone.

• *Frank Beamer (25) and Ron Davidson (24) try to bring down FSU receiver Ron Sellers.*

Stafford's 30-yard pass to Tommy Francisco was the key play in the drive. Stafford connected with Ken Barefoot on the TD pass, with 2:45 left in the first quarter. Jon Utin booted the extra point to give Tech a 9-0 lead.

FSU came back in the second quarter with a 89-yard scoring drive. Pajcic threw to Sellers five times for 55 yards on the drive.

After reaching the Tech 3, Moreman scored the first of his three touchdowns. Pete Roberts' extra-point kick, with 3:52 left before the half, narrowed Tech's lead to 9-7.

The Seminoles would come out passing in the second half.

On their first drive, Pajcic connected on 5 of six passes for 54 yards to give FSU a 14-9 lead. Moreman scored on a 7-yard pass with 10:32 left in the third quarter.

Minutes later, Loria made his electrifying 80-yard punt return for a TD to put Tech back on top. Utin's point-after kick made it 16-14.

Ron Davidson then recovered Tech's on-side kick at the FSU 47 on the next play.

Stafford threw two passes to Tommy Groom for first downs and then connected on a 10-yard pass to Francisco for the touchdown. Utin added the extra point and Tech led, 23-14.

Pajcic hit the airlanes for 86 yards to get the score close again, 23-21.

Whitley's interception in the final quarter wrapped up the win for Tech.

| Florida State | 0 | 7 | 14 | 0 | — | 21 |
| Virginia Tech | 9 | 0 | 14 | 0 | — | 23 |

Francisco's 6 Touchdowns Crush VMI

ROANOKE, Nov. 24, 1966 — Virginia Tech's Tommy Francisco pounded Virginia Military Institute with six touchdowns as the Gobblers routed the longtime rival Keydets, 70-12, today at Victory Stadium.

The Gobblers scored twice in the second quarter without running a play to take a 21-0 lead.

The 70-12 score, however, could have been worse.

The Gobblers put together 516 yards on offense, including 360 on the ground.

Francisco, the 6-foot-1, 190-pound senior from Damascus, Va., ripped for 132 yards on 32 carries.

He scored on runs of 1, 26, 3, 1, 3 and 1 yard, which set a school record for touchdowns in one game and tied Tech season records for most TD's (14) and points scored.

The victory gave the Gobblers an 8-1-1 season record and a seven-game winning streak.

Tech used everything in its playbook against the Keydets. The Gobblers twice used the on-side kickoff — and got the ball both times. They also faked a field goal, using a pass to pick up a first down that eventually led to a touchdown.

But Tech's power sweeps and off-tackle runs were the keys to victory. The Gobblers roared for 315 yards and a 35-6 lead at halftime. Francisco rushed for 95 of those yards.

Tech's passing game, however, was less than spectacular.

The Gobbler defense kept VMI quarterback Hill Ellett on the run. Frequent blitzes by Tech defensive linemen Clarence Culpepper and Sal Garcia rarely gave Andy Bowling time to get off a pass. On his first attempt, Bowling was thrown for a six-yard loss.

The Keydets finished with 197 yards on offense, including 46 yards on the ground against the No. 6 rushing defense in the country.

Ellett, completed 11 of 29 attempts for 142 yards. He had two passes intercepted.

Tech turned a recovered fumble by Bowling and an interception by Frank Beamer into a pair of second-half touchdowns.

The Gobblers scored the first time it had the ball after marching 76 yards in 10 plays. Francisco ran for 23 yards to set up the score and then finished the drive with a 1-yard run for the TD.

Tech scored again early in the second quarter with an 8-play, 75-yard drive. Quarterback Tommy Stafford dashed for 37 yards on a rollout on the big play of the series. Stafford then passed to end Ken Barefoot for a 6-yard TD to give Tech a 14-0 lead.

Ron Davidson recovered an on-side kick to give Tech the ball at the VMI 45. The Gobblers scored in four plays, with Francisco sweeping right end for a 26-yard touchdown romp.

A fake field goal set up the next Tech touchdown.

• *Gobblers halfback George Constantinides (44) ran four yards for a fourth-quarter TD.*

Stafford passed to Rick Piland for 9 yards on the play. Then Francisco smashed three yards for the TD to give the Gobblers a 28-0 lead.

Tech scored again on a 9-yard pass from Eddy Barker to Barefoot to take a 35-0 lead.

VMI then responded with a 57-yard drive before halftime. Ellett's 32-yard pass to Jim Breckenridge set up the score. Ellett threw 31 yards to Cap Easterly for the TD. After a missed point-after kick, Tech led, 35-6.

Bob Schmalzriedt's blitz of Stafford forced an interception by Tony Gentile in the third quarter. Gentile returned the ball 39 yards to the Tech 11. Ellett then passed to Breckenridge for a 3-yard touchdown to narrow the score to 35-12.

Francisco scored again on a 1-yard plunge after Bowling recovered a VMI fumbled punt at the Keydet 23.

After Randy Treadwell recovered another on-side kick at the VMI 35, Francisco scored his fifth touchdown on a 3-yard run to give the Gobblers a 49-12 lead.

Barker connected on a pair of passes to Piland for 60 yards and a 21-yard run by Rusty Fife took Tech to the VMI 4. George Constantinides then ran the final yardage for the TD.

Third-string Tech quarterback Fred Cobb drove the Gobblers 50 yards for another touchdown. Cobb's 16-yard pass to Danny Cupp capped the drive to give Tech a 63-12 lead.

Beamer's interception set up Tech's final touchdown. Francisco scored five plays later on a 1-yard dive. John Utin booted his 10th straight extra point, which set a school record to wrap up the scoring.

Virginia Tech	7	28	14	21	— 70
VMI	0	6	6	0	— 12

Miami Turns Back Gobblers in Liberty Bowl

MEMPHIS, Dec. 10, 1966 — Quarterback Bill Miller hit James Cox on a 38-yard fourth-quarter pass play today to set up the winning touchdown that gave Miami a 14-7 win over Virginia Tech in the Liberty Bowl.

The Gobblers held Miami scoreless in the first half. But in the second half, fullback Doug McGee and halfback Joe Mira managed to open up the Hurricanes' attack and pull out the victory.

McGee plunged over from the Tech 1-yard line to break the 7-7 tie four plays after the Miller-to-Cox aerial.

Miami's first touchdown came on a seven-yard pass from Miller to Mira in the third quarter to cap a drive that started on Miami's 47. Ray Harris booted both of the Hurricanes' extra points.

Tech scored midway through the second quarter, with Tommy Francisco running over on a 1-yard dive for the TD to cap a five-play drive that started on the Miami 21 when Jimmy Richards blocked a Bobby Stokes' punt. John Utin's extra-point kick gave the Gobblers a 7-0 lead.

The Gobblers, who entered the game as 10-point underdogs, passed from their 13 on the game's first play — and then they opened up.

Before the contest ended, the 25,012 fans and a nationwide television audience had seen such rarities as a quick kick, a Statue of Liberty play attempt that failed, and a quarterback sneak attempt to run a play without a huddle early in the fourth quarter. The play ended in a penalty for the Gobblers after their line was ruled offsides.

At times, when the gambles worked, the Gobblers looked like a miniature Alabama team. Virginia Tech's coach, Jerry Claiborne, went to Tech six years ago after playing for Bryant at Kentucky and serving as an assistant to Bryant at Texas A&M and Alabama. When he left Alabama, Claiborne obviously took Bryant's football playbook.

Miami played conservative football, content on waiting for the breaks.

Tech dominated the first half, smothering a Miami attack that had beaten Orange Bowl bound Florida, Southern Cal and Georgia during the regular season.

The Hurricanes had the ball seven times in the first half, but it seemed that every time a Hurricane hit the line, Tech's all-American safety, Frank Loria, was there to meet him. The Gobblers held Miami to just 16 yards total offense in the first two quarters, and did not allow a Hurricane inside their 30.

Miami entered the contest with a 7-2-1 regular-season record. Tech had been 8-1-1, including a win over Florida State.

Miami	0	0	7	7	— 14
Virginia Tech	7	0	0	0	— 7

• *Tech scored early against Miami, but the Hurricanes pulled out a fourth-quarter win.*

Frank Loria: Virginia Tech's Greatest Gridiron Hero

Frank Loria got to Virginia Tech because most of the major colleges in the South, Midwest and East thought he was too small, including his home state school of West Virginia.

Loria was an all-state halfback and captain at Notre Dame High in Clarksburg, W. Va. He was 5-9 ½, 175 lbs. And somewhat slow, running the 40-yard dash in 4.8.

He was a quiet leader, letting his actions on the football field and off the field speak for themselves.

He was named an all-American in 1966 by The Associated Press and the Football Writers Association of America and was named to six all-America teams in 1967.

Loria would start every game during his three-year career, 1965-67, and played every defensive down as a sophomore in 1965.

His coach, Jerry Claiborne, described Loria's ability to be at the right spot on a play: "He was practically a coach on the field. He could diagnose a play and know where it was going."

His backfield coach during his first two seasons was Bobby Collins, who later became the head coach at Southern Miss and at SMU. Collins recalled, "Frankie did things that you can't teach a player."

Lee Royer, Loria's secondary coach in 1967, added, "Sometimes, we thought he heard little voices telling him where the play is going."

• *Frank Loria, an all-America safety in 1966 and '67.*

• *Frank Loria's on-the-field heroics from 1965 to 1967 set the standard for all Virginia Tech players.*

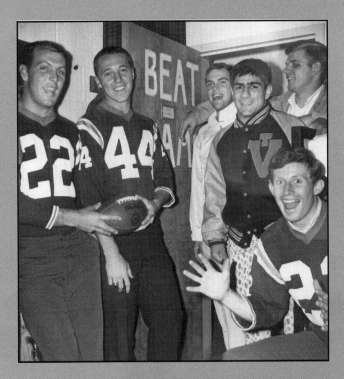

Loria holds the Tech record for the longest punt return after racing 95 yards against Miami in 1967. He returned three punts for touchdowns in 1966 — distances of 80, 65 and 80 yards. His 61 punt returns over three seasons totaled 813 yards.

One of Loria's heroics is best decribed in the following:

After the first three games of the 1966 season, Tech's record was 1-1-1 and the Hokies were playing Kentucky. The Hokies were ahead, 7-0, and it was early in the fourth quarter.

Kentucky was at the Tech 4-yard line, trying to tie the score. On his own, Loria decided to blitz Wildcat quarterback Roger Walz. He threw Walz for a 2-yard loss, which eventually stopped the drive and saved the game for Tech. It also set in motion Tech's seven-game winning streak which led to a Liberty Bowl berth against Miami.

Afterward, Claiborne said, "That Loria has the guts of a cat burgler."

In the 1966 Liberty Bowl with the Hurricanes, Loria was voted the game's most valuable player.

Against Kansas State in 1967, Loria intercepted a pass, recovered a fumble, made two touchdown-saving tackles, deflected a TD pass and blitzed a quarterback for a 9-yard loss.

He was also voted an Academic all-American in 1967 and played in the East-West Shrine game, the Hula Bowl and the Coaches All-American Game.

After graduating, he became an assistant at Marshall University. On Nov. 14, 1970, the Marshall team and its coaching staff, including Loria, was killed in a plane crash. He was only 23 years old.

• Frank Loria dashes for a TD after intercepting a pass against Miami in 1967.

Tech Explodes, Crushes No. 18 Seminoles

TALLAHASSEE, Fla., Nov. 2, 1968 — Virginia Tech turned Florida State's vaunted aerial attack to the Gobblers' advantage tonight before 31,342 fans tonight at Doak Campbell Stadium and handed the No. 18-ranked Seminoles a crushing 40-22 setback.

Tech intercepted six FSU passes — two more than had been intercepted by Seminole opponents in FSU's first five games — and used three to launch touchdown drives in the first half. A fourth touchdown came after the Gobblers recovered a fumbled lateral pass.

The victory left the Gobblers with a 4-3 season record. Florida State, which has yielded 68 points in its last two games, is 4-2.

Gator Bowl scouts watching Florida State saw little they could report favorably about the Seminoles in the contest.

For the second week in a row, Tech supplemented its tight defense with both a rushing and passing attack, which included unusually efficient execution of the draw play, the end-around and the play-action pass.

Tech's opportunists took advantage of every scoring chance except one in the first half as they rolled to a 31-7 halftime advantage. Jack Simcsak missed a 55-yard field goal try as time was running out in the half.

Tech's defense got its first test following the opening kickoff when the Seminoles rolled 60 yards in nine plays — aided by an illegal use of hands penalty — to the Tech 20. On fourth-and-8, Grant Guthrie attempted a 37-yard field goal, but it faded to the right.

Tech's newly-found offense asserted itself immediately with Ken Edwards keying the attack. He picked up 50 yards in his first three carries and 59 of the 68 yards gained by the Gobblers as they set the stage for a 32-yard field goal by Simcsak. It came with 6:09 left in the first quarter.

Two plays after the ensuing kickoff, defensive back Ron Davidson pulled in a pass thrown by FSU's highly touted quarterback, Bill Cappleman. He returned it 15 yards to the FSU 15.

Four plays later, Terry Smoot ran over left tackle for three yards and a TD. Simcsak's extra-point kick gave Tech a 10-0 lead with 3:44 left in the opening quarter.

Cappleman threw for 67 of the 80 yards that FSU marched to a touchdown, which came on the first play of the second quarter. The scoring play came on a 34-yard pass from Cappleman to tight end Jim Tyson.

Tech, hit by two illegal-procedure penalties in a row, was forced to punt after receiving the kickoff. But, when Cappleman took to the air again, Mike Widger pulled in the first of two interceptions he

• *Ken Edwards ran 88 yards for Tech's third TD.*

third touchdown. Simcsak's extra-point kick made it 24-7 with 7:41 left in the half.

Edwards run tied a record for the longest run from scrimmage against FSU.

Only 12 seconds elapsed until the Gobblers had another score. Tommy Warren took the kickoff and attempted to lateral to Gary Pajcic, but the ball was fumbled and Tech linebacker John Ivanac fell on it at the FSU 10.

On the next play, George Constantinides burst through the line for the TD. The Gobblers led, 35-7, at halftime.

Tech's offense continued to roll in high gear as the third quarter began. The Gobblers rolled 80 yards in 15 plays to the FSU 3, but a 17-yard Simcsak field goal failed.

Two plays later, Widger made his second interception of a Cappleman pass, carrying it from FSU 30 to the 23. Four plays later, Simcsak booted a 37-yard field goal.

Cappleman then completed two passes for 35 yards and another personal foul penalty against Tech put the ball on the Tech 20. But four Cappleman passes went awry and Tech began a 59-yard drive that was later aborted when Constantinides' fumble was recovered by Doug Gurr.

Cappleman put the ball in the air on a 72-yard march that ended with a FSU touchdown just as the fourth quarter began. Cappleman threw to Tyson for the final five yards.

Midway through the period, Lenny Smith intercepted a Cappleman pass on the Tech 42. Edwards ran for 19 yards and a personal foul penalty against FSU were key plays in the 58-yard drive. Kincaid rolled right around end for the last 11 yards and the TD.

In the final minutes, FSU launched a 60-yard drive that culminated with Sub quarterback Tommy Warren throwing a 25-yard pass to Pajcic in the end zone. Warren connected with Mike Gray for the two-point play to wrap up the scoring.

had for the night and returned for seven yards to the FSU 28.

Two running plays picked up a first down to the 14 before Tech quarterback Al Kincaid threw over the right side to Edwards, who caught the ball on the 2-yard line and scored.

Florida State, aided by a 17-yard Cappleman pass to split end Billy Cox and a 15-yard personal foul penalty on the same play, moved 45 yards to the Tech 35. This time another Cappleman pass was intercepted by Lenny Smith on the Tech 10 and returned to the Gobblers' 12.

On the first play, Edwards slid off left tackle and with three FSU defenders chasing him — and losing ground all of the time — ran 88 yards for Tech's

Virginia Tech	10	21	3	6	—	40
Florida State	0	7	0	15	—	22

Gobblers Fumble Win to Ole Miss in Liberty Bowl

MEMPHIS, Dec. 14, 1968 — Johnny Vaught's Ole Miss Rebels battled back from a flurry of early scoring by Virginia Tech this afternoon and rolled to a 34-17 win over the fumbling Gobblers in an explosive Liberty Bowl duel.

The Rebels wiped out a 17-0 deficit behind the passing of all-American quarterback Archie Manning and an alert defense that pounced on three Virginia Tech fumbles and intercepted two passes.

Manning, a lanky sophomore described by Vaught as one of his best, ignited the comeback with TD passes of 21 and 23 yards in the second quarter.

Steve Hindman, a halfback, put the Rebels ahead to stay on the opening play of the second half with a 79-yard touchdown run. The Rebels, who were playing in their 12th straight bowl game, clinched the win in the final quarter when Bob Bailey bolted 70 yards for a touchdown with an intercepted pass and Van Brown kicked field goals from 46 and 26 yards.

The Gobblers, who had not fumbled in their last five games and boasted a season record of 7-3, swept to the lead with some surprising razzle-dazzle. They startled the Rebels and a record crowd of 46,206, which included Vice President-elect Spiro Agnew, with a "muddle huddle" that produced a touchdown on their second running play.

Ken Edwards dashed 58 yards for the score on a play that started with the Gobblers huddling on the line of scrimmage. Al Kincaid, the quarterback, walked to the ball and casually pitched it to Edwards.

The touchdown took only 27 seconds. Tech scored again two minutes later on Terry Smoot's 7-yard run that was set up by Manning's fumble.

The Gobblers widened the gap on a 29-yard field goal by Jack Simcsak later in the first quarter, which put Tech up, 17-0.

Tech completed only one pass this afternoon — and that completion produced only a 2-yard gain in the final minutes.

Vaught said that a Virginia Tech gamble that backfired after the Gobblers' field goal was the key to Ole Miss' comeback.

Tech tried an on-side kick after the field goal and the Rebels recovered on the Gobbler 49. Manning & Co. needed only seven plays to produce their first touchdown. They then proceeded to pull away.

Tech pounded through Ole Miss' defense for 330 yards rushing, but the lack of a passing attack was fatal for the Gobblers' comeback hopes.

Edwards, who was moved to fullback at mid-season, gained 119 yards in 12 carries for Tech. Smoot picked up 91 yards on 21 carries.

Virginia Tech	17	0	0	0	—	17
Ole Miss	0	14	7	13	—	35

• *Halfback Terry Smoot (44), who led the Gobblers in rushing from 1967-69, dives for a TD.*

Jerry Claiborne: Builder of the Tech Legacy

Jerry Claiborne arrived in Blacksburg in 1961 from the Bear Bryant school of coaching at Alabama, Texas A&M and Kentucky, hoping to build the Hokies into another college football mecca.

A native of Hopkinsville, Ky., he replaced another Bryant disciple, Frank Moseley, who had coached with Bryant at Maryland and Kentucky and had been at the Tech helm for nine seasons before moving upstairs to become athletic director. Moseley's record at Tech was 54-42-4 — the best for a Hokies' coach at that time.

In 10 seasons at Tech, Claiborne won more games than Moseley and became the winningest football coach in Hokies' history. His record was 61-39-2.

He led Tech to the Southern Conference championship in 1963 and to the Liberty Bowl in 1966 and 1968.

He had two losing seasons in 1969 and 1970 that led to his firing.

Claiborne started off 0-5 in 1970, but his team rallied to a 5-1 record in the last six games.

He left to coach the defense at Colorado in 1971, then was named head coach at the University of Maryland in 1972.

In 10 seasons with the Terrapins, Claiborne's teams posted a record of 77-37-3, playing in seven bowl games.

On Dec. 16, 1981, his alma mater, Kentucky, called and Claiborne departed College Park for Lexington to clean up a scandal-ridden program. In eight seasons with the Wildcats, his record was only 41-46-3.

Kentucky played well in Claiborne's early years, going 6-5-1 in 1983 and 9-3 in 1984. The Wildcats played in the Hall of Fame Bowl at the end of both seasons.

He finished at Kentucky with a 6-5 record.

When he retired, his overall record was 179-122-8 in 28 seasons, the fourth winningest among active Division I coaches.

He was named coach of the year in three conferences — the Southern in 1963, the Atlantic Coast in 1973, 1975 and 1976, and the SEC in 1983.

Claiborne, who began his coaching career in 1950 as a coach at Augusta Military Academy in Defiance, Va., was voted into the College Football Hall of Fame in 1999.

The Claiborne File

School	W	L	T
Virginia Tech	61	39	2
Maryland	77	37	3
Kentucky	41	46	3
Total	179	122	8

• *Tech coach Jerry Claiborne   (right) huddles on the sideline with his quarterback, Al Kincaid (11).*

Strock Boots Tech to Win

BLACKSBURG, Oct. 14, 1972 — The "Other Strock" pulled off today perhaps the biggest win ever on Tech's campus by defeating No. 19 Oklahoma State, 34-32, and gave 36,000 Gobblers in Lane Stadium a Homecoming that they will long remember.

Dave Strock booted the 18-yard field goal with 12 seconds left that ensured the win. Earlier in the day, he booted his longest — a 53-yarder.

His brother, Don Strock, put on a spectacular performance at quarterback. He connected on 20 of 40 attempts for 355 yards and a pair of touchdowns.

Oklahoma State entered the contest as the No. 2 rushing team in the country. The Cowboys piled up 356 yards on the ground against Tech.

A fumble by OSU fullback George Palmer, who had 128 yards on 29 carries, with 1:15 left to play set up Strock's winning kick.

Tech's Donnie Sprouse fell on the loose ball.

James Barber got the ball to the OSU 1-yard line.

"We waited to call time out (their last)," Tech coach Charlie Coffey explained.

With his third opportunity in less than two minutes, Strock's kick was true and Tech's No. 2 citizen from Warwick, Pa., won the game.

Oklahoma State	14	9	0	3	—	32
Virginia Tech	7	17	0	10	—	34

• Dave Strock's 18-yard field goal gave Virginia Tech a 34-32 win.

Don Strock: The Quarterback With a Rocket Arm

Don Strock's name can be found atop every passing record in the Virginia Tech football record book. Yet he almost never had the opportunity to be the Hokies' starting quarterback.

As a sophomore, he spent most of the season as the team's third-team quarterback.

Then enter new Tech coach Charlie Coffey and his offensive coordinator Dan Henning. They brought with them a new pro-style offense that suited Strock's talents.

As a junior, with Henning as his tutor, Strock passed for 195 completions on 356 attempts for 2,577 yards and 12 touchdowns.

In his senior year, Strock opened up, completing 228 passes on 427 attempts for 3,243 yards and 16 TD's.

He would finish his career with 457 completions on 875 attempts for 6,009 yards and 29 touchdowns.

The Strock File

	Att	Comp	Yards	TD	Int
1970	46	17	189	1	1
1971	402	212	2,577	12	19
1972	427	228	3,243	16	27
Total	875	457	6,009	29	47

• *Don Strock threw for nearly 5,800 yards in two seasons and led the country in passing his senior season.*

Tech's Late Goal Line Stand Stuns Auburn

AUBURN, Ala., Oct. 4, 1975 — Virginia Tech's startling 23-16 win over Auburn this afternoon is perhaps the biggest moment to date in Jimmy Sharpe's tenure since he left the prosperity of Bear Bryant's staff at Alabama to direct the Gobblers prior to last season.

"I'm shaking all over," he beamed minutes after his Gobblers stunned Auburn and a rain-soaked crowd of 45,000 at Jordan-Hare Stadium. "That was the greatest display of guts and determination I've ever been associated with."

It was Tech's greatest road victory ever and biggest upset since a 20-11 win over Florida State in 1964.

For Auburn coach Ralph (Shug) Jordan the loss was perhaps his lowest point ever and the lowest in Auburn history.

"Tonight," he said grimly, "Auburn football is about as low as it's ever been. It wasn't this was low when I came to Auburn in 1951. We're down mentally, and the road ahead looks dark and ominous."

Picked by many sportswriters to finish in the Top 10, Auburn has yet to win a game in Jordan's 25th and final season. The Tigers are 0-3-1 so far.

Tech's defense made sure of the final outcome for Sharpe.

In the final two minutes of the game, Auburn moved from its own 20 to the Tech 5, where the Tigers had first-and-goal.

Two running plays and a pass later, Auburn was still on the Tech 5.

The whole game came down to just one play, with 37 seconds left to play.

On fourth down, Auburn quarterback Clyde Baumgartner dropped back to find an open receiver. Unable to locate one, he rolled left to run around end.

Baumgartner, who had replaced starting quarterback Phil Gargis on the last drive, was met by several Tech defenders, who drove him out of bounds at the Tech 4 to preserve the win.

"A lot of people had kissed off our chances this week. They thought it was just a matter of how many people we'd get beat up.

"We had been in our regular goal line defense on the first three plays (of the goal line stand)," he added. "But one of my assistants (Buddy Bennett), suggested we go back to our basic defense on fourth down. It gives more support to the outside,"

Tech defensive tackle Tom Beasley said afterward, "I think about six of us got him (Baumgartner) on the play. We were just looking for anything on that play."

The Gobblers, running from a wishbone attack that Sharpe had brought from Alabama, rolled to 337 yards rushing.

Halfback Roscoe Coles rambled for 139 yards on 14 carries, including an 89-yard TD run on the second play of the second half to put Tech on top, 16-10.

• *Roscoe Coles' 89-yard TD in the third quarter gave Tech a 16-13 lead against Auburn.*

Gobblers quarterback Phil Rogers turned in a super performance, running for 128 yards and a touchdown and passing for 68 yards and a TD.

Tech is now 2-2 for the season.

Auburn scored first on a 53-yard field goal by Neil O'Donoghue in the opening quarter.

Early in the second quarter, Auburn drove to the Tech 2 but a Kenny Burks' fumble halted the effort.

Tech got going minutes later and marched 80 yards in 17 plays, with Rogers passing to his favorite receiver Steve Galloway alone in the end zone. A bad snap on the extra-point kick left tech with a 6-3 lead.

Auburn struck right back, driving 70 yards in eight plays. Burks scored on a 6-yard run with 1:42 left in the half to take a 10-6 lead.

The Gobblers, however, were determined to light up the scoreboard once more before halftime. Tech drove to the Auburn 3, but had to settle for a Wayne Lattimer field goal that left Auburn ahead, 10-9.

Coles got loose on his 89-yard TD run early in the third quarter to give tech a 16-10 lead.

Auburn responded with a 47-yard O'Donoghue field goal to make it 16-13 midway in the third quarter.

Tech kept it rolling by driving 70 yards in eight plays, with Rogers scoring on an 8-yard run to put Tech up, 23-13.

O'Donoghue added a 30-yard field goal early in the final quarter to make it 23-16.

Virginia Tech	0	9	14	0	—	23
Auburn	3	7	3	3	—	16

Latimer's 61-Yard Field Goal Defeats Florida State

BLACKSBURG, Oct. 11, 1975 — Wayne Latimer, who was sent into the game on the advice of one of Jimmy Sharpe's assistants with 7:51 left in the game, booted a 61-yard field goal to give Virginia Tech a 13-10 lead and the eventual win over Florida State tonight.

Latimer, a 5-9, 170 lb. senior from Meadowbrook High School, kicked a hard, booming kick, with the wind, and it sailed through the uprights to send a Homecoming crowd of 38,000 at Lane Stadium into a wild frenzy.

The kick set a school record, breaking the one Dave Strock set after booting a 57-yarder against Southern Miss in 1972, and gave Tech three straight wins for the first time since 1970.

"It wasn't exactly how we planned the script," joked Sharpe. "Coach (Jack) White was in the press box. He works with the kickers and he felt Wayne could do it.

"I had already called for a punt, but he got on the head phones and said, 'He can do it, he can do it.' "

Latimer didn't need to be coaxed.

"The only thing that was going through my mind was, 'Hit it good,' " explained Latimer, whose previous best had been a 55-yarder against Virginia two years ago.

Lattimer knocked the ensuing kickoff out of the end zone, giving FSU the ball at their 20.

Quarterback Clyde Walker then threw three straight completions of 16, 44 and 17 yards to split end Mike Sherman to march the Seminoles to the Tech 11.

On fourth-and-four with 2:59 left in the game, FSU decided against a field goal that would have tied the game and opted to go for the touchdown.

"Our players didn't need a tie, we needed a win," said Seminoles coach Darrell Mudra.

Tech defensive Tom Beasley tried to sack Walker while he attempted to pass. Evading the rush, he passed to halfback Rudy Thomas who made the catch two yards out of the end zone."

Tech got the ball again and ran down the clock. Punter Bruce McDaniel let loose a 68-yard punt that left FSU on their 5-yard line with less than a minute remaining.

After two losses at the beginning of the season, Tech is now 3-2 for first time since 1972 when the Gobblers went 6-4-1.

"This winning can become contagious," said Sharpe, in his second season at the helm. "Coming back in the second half is the hard way to do it, but we'll take it."

Tech scored on its first drive of the game when Latimer kicked a 37-yard field goal to give the Gobblers a 3-0 lead.

The Seminoles ended a nine-quarter scoring drought with 4:12 left in the second quarter when Walker dove for the final yard of a 62-yard drive to

• *Phil Rogers (40), who played both quarterback and halfback, rips off-tackle against the FSU defense.*

put Florida State ahead, 7-3.

Tech was unable to get outside on the wishbone in the first half, gaining only 84 yards on 35 carries.

In the third quarter, FSU drove 47 yards to the Tech 12 before Keith Singletary hit a 30-yard field goal to up the Seminoles' lead to 10-3.

The Gobblers began playing defense late in the third quarter, stopping FSU on three straight series.

Tech's offense found new life and drove to the FSU 15. Latimer was wide on a 32-yard field goal.

Tech later took over on the FSU 38 after a pass interference call against FSU. Two plays later,

Roscoe Coles ripped down the sidelines for a 36-yard TD run to tie the score at 10-10.

Late in the game, Tech drove from its 37 to the FSU 44. When fourth down came, Latimer made his game-winning appearance.

Florida State	0	7	3	0	—	10
Virginia Tech	3	0	0	10	—	13

Tech's Wild Fourth Quarter Defeats Houston

HOUSTON, Nov. 8, 1975 — In one of the wildest games ever played in the Astrodome, Virginia Tech exploded for a pair of touchdowns in the final quarter tonight within 1:06 to overcome Houston's lead and take a 34-28 win.

The Hokies improved their record to 6-3 and assured itself of a winning season.

A crowd of 17,350 on Band Night watched the two teams commit a total of 15 turnovers. Houston had 9 of these.

Quarterback Bubba McGallion's one-yard run and a 2-point play tied the game at 22-22 for Houston.

On the Cougars' next series, Charles Lynch fumbled at the Houston 40 and Rick Razano recovered at the Houston 46.

Three plays later, Phil Rogers, who played both quarterback and halfback in the Hokies' wishbone offense, turned the corner on the right side and raced 38 yards into the end zone to give Tech a 28-22 lead.

Rogers, who was playing quarterback on the game-breaking play, had 168 yards rushing. This total gave Rogers 2,228 in career yards rushing, breaking Terry Smoot's all-time rushing record of 2,116 yards.

Latimer, whose 23-yard field goal in the third quarter set a school record of 23 career field goals, missed the extra point with 4:59 left to play.

McGallion tried to get Houston back in the game by passing. But linebacker Doug Thacker grabbed Tech's fourth interception of the game and ran 34 yards to reach the Houston end zone with 3:53 left. Latimer again missed the point-after kick, leaving Tech ahead, 34-22.

Houston, which lost five of seven fumbles, scored once more when McGallion's connected on a 15-yard TD pass to Eddie Foster with nine seconds left.

The win was Tech's first in five tries against Houston and avenged a 49-12 loss last season.

The Hokies amassed 365 yards rushing and 439 yards in total offense against Houston. Roscoe Coles had 90 and Paul Adams had 80.

Tech's only two passes went for touchdowns, both to Steve Galloway.

The first half was dominated by Tech. The Hokies scored in the first quarter on a 9-play drive after recovering a fumble at the Houston 40. Adams went over right guard from the Houston 1 for the score.

Nineteen seconds later, Tech scored again after recovering a Houston fumble at the Cougars' 27.

Rogers faked into the line, then dropped back and passed to Galloway, who was wide open at the goal line to give Tech a 13-0 lead. Latimer's extra-point kick was blocked by Houston's Ken Perry.

Virginia Tech	13	0	9	12	—	34
Houston	0	0	14	14	—	28

• *Phil Rogers (40), who rushed for 168 yards, broke Tech's all-time rushing record set earlier by Terry Smoot.*

Lamie's Bomb in Final Second Defeats W&M

BLACKSBURG, Sept. 30, 1978 — With .08 left on the Lane Stadium scoreboard and William & Mary ahead, 19-15, Hokies quarterback David Lamie went to the air one last time, lofted a 50-yard spiral to end Ron Zollicoffer, who outfought several W&M defenders at the goal line, and Tech pulled out one of its most sensational thrillers.

Paul Engle kicked the extra point to give Tech a 22-19 win which knocked W&M from the unbeaten ranks.

Zollicoffer's game-winning catch brought a nail-biting conclusion. As the Tech receiver fell across the goal line, he fumbled the ball as he hit the ground. The officials, however, ruled that Zollicoffer had possession of the ball in W&M end zone before the ball was knocked loose.

The 34,000 in Lane Stadium, who were all standing, went wild after the official's decision was announced.

W&M had taken the lead with 1:29 left to play when the Indians' quarterback, Tom Rozantz, threw a 59-yard bomb to third-string receiver Ed Schielfelbein. Steve Libassi booted the extra point to put W&M ahead, 19-15.

"I heard a lot of boos out there today, but when Zolly came up with the ball I heard a lot of cheers," said Lamie, who completed 8 of 21 passes for 160 yards and two interceptions against the Indians.

"It was one of those 'Hail Mary' passes that somebody had to go up and get."

The winning pass was a deep post to the sophomore wide receiver — and a rare pass that Zollicoffer did not have to stop and come back to. Lamie and Zollicoffer had run a similar route earlier and felt that they could beat W&M's coverage.

"I watched for it and saw him release when I made my out cut," Zollicoffer explained. "I saw it (the ball) hang and knew I at least had a chance to get under it. I don't think I ever broke stride until the ball was in my hands."

The catch was Zollicoffer's only one of the day.

Tech is now 2-2 for the season. W&M is 3-1.

The Hokies posted 400 yards of total offense, including 240 yards rushing. Tailback Kenny Lewis piled up 147 yards on the ground and two TD's.

"We did our celebrating a couple plays too early," said W&M coach Jim Root, whose team had celebrated Schielfelbein's touchdown throw to take the lead.

"The problem with my football team was it had to play under tremendous adversity the entire game."

Four times the Indians took over in Tech territory and came away with points on all four occasions.

Libassi booted a 47-yard field goal following a fumble recovery at the Tech 37 in the second quarter. A little later, Tech's short punt gave W&M the ball at the Tech 41. A 40-yard bomb from Rozantz to Indians

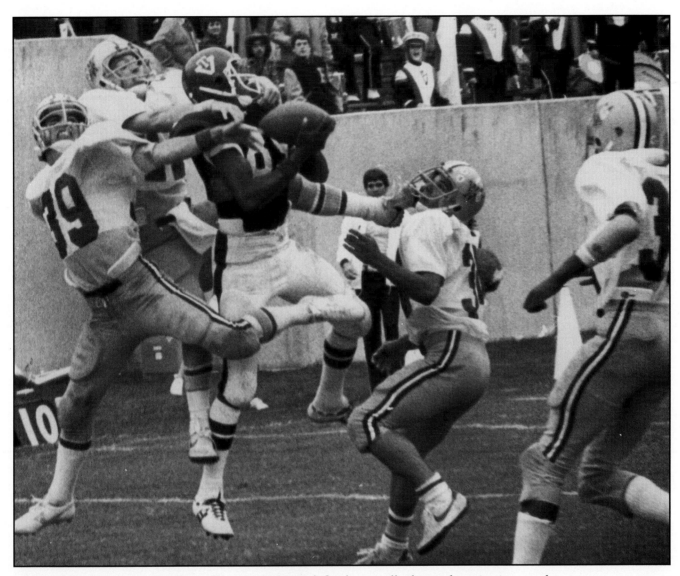

• *Ron Zellicoffer, after fending off several W&M defenders, pulls down the winning catch.*

receiver Joe Manderfield put the ball at the Tech 1-yard line. Tailback Andy Banks ran the final yard for the touchdown which gave W&M a 9-0 lead.

Tech, who gained only 82 yards in the first half, was a different team in the second half.

"In the first half, I didn't do a good job reading the defense," admitted Lamie. "The entire offense wasn't executing."

In the third quarter, Tech marched 67 yards for a touchdown, with Lewis running 3 yards for the TD.

Paul Tyner intercepted a Lamie pass at the Tech 44. A pass interference call ended the drive, but

Libassi was able to get a 41-yard field goal to put the Indians up, 12-7.

Tech got the ball at the W&M 46 and scored in six plays, with Lewis running 8 yards for the TD. Afterward, Lamie's 2-point run gave Tech a 15-12 lead with 10:59 left to play.

Then came the pair of touchdowns that both teams made in the final two minutes.

William & Mary	0	9	3	7	—	19
Virginia Tech	0	0	7	15	—	22

65

Bruce Smith: Bigger Than a Mountain

When Virginia Tech coach Bill Dooley first saw Bruce Smith, Smith was in a basketball uniform playing for Booker T. Washington High in Norfolk, Va.

"You could see what a great athlete he was," Dooley said. "He wasn't hard to pick out. It was like picking a Miss America from a group of ordinary-looking girls.

"I'm watching him and I'm saying to myself, 'I do believe I could coach this youngster.' Bruce could run and he could jump, and he was about 6-3, 240 pounds."

Dooley was off by 30 pounds.

"I weighed 270 then," Smith explained. "I could dunk the ball with either hand."

Smith could have gone on to be another Charles Barkley, but instead he went to Tech and became the school's greatest football player.

He won the Outland Trophy in 1984, which is given to the country's best interior lineman by the Football Writers Association of America.

In his four-year career in Hokieland, Smith made 71 tackles behind the line of scrimmage for losses totaling 504 yards. Overall, he had 167 tackles.

In 1983 he had 55 tackles, including 31 behind the line of scrimmage for 223 yards in losses — 22 of these were quarterback sacks — while earning all-America honors.

In 1984, despite being double- and triple-teamed, he got 16 sacks and nine other tackles behind the line of scrimmage. He had a total of 69 tackles and was a consensus all-American.

Smith ran a 4.7 40-yard dash while in Blacksburg, and his competitive fire while on defense is legendary.

"Bruce never, never gives in," said Dooley. "He plays the fourth quarter like he plays the first quarter."

Smith never lacked the confidence to be great when he arrived at Tech.

"As a freshman I had thoughts in my mind of being better than anyone else who has ever played here," he said. "I remember other players telling me, 'I wish I could be in your shoes,' or 'I'd like to trade places with you.'

"I had the ability to excel at the game of football. I knew that. I sat back and thought about that and realized that even though I had all of these abilities it was up to me to put them to good use."

So worked to become the best player to ever play for the maroon and orange. He became the greatest player to ever play in Virginia.

"I'd tell any young football player that whenever you set high goals for yourself, it's always hard. Nothing is given to you. You have to work, sweat and sometimes cry. In the end, it's worth it when it's time to receive the things you deserve."

Smith was the first player picked in the 1995 NFL draft by the Buffalo Bills. He has earned All-Pro 11 times and played in four Super Bowls.

• Bruce Smith, a 2-time all-American, won the
Outland Trophy as the country's best lineman.

Hokies End 32-Year Drought With Clemson

CLEMSON, S.C., Sept. 13, 1986 — Virginia Tech upset the Clemson Tigers in Memorial Stadium tonight, 20-14, for the first time since 1954. Their effort not only quieted the 78,000 Clemson fans in the stands but also buried the ghosts of previous Tech losses.

The Tigers (0-1) hadn't lost a home opener since 1977, when Maryland won, 21-14.

Tech scored in the first quarter against Clemson for the first time in seven games. They also scored more than 17 points against the Tigers for the first time in their 22-game series.

Tech got on the scoreboard in the first quarter after blocking a punt in the Clemson end zone to take a 7-0 lead.

Tigers punter Bill Spiers, a sophomore, was playing in his first game. A baseball player on the Clemson squad, he answered Tiger Coach Danny Ford's newspaper ad for a punter. His first kick went 41 yards, but the second was blocked.

The Hokies passed for 242 yards and one TD, taking advantage of the Tigers' seldom pass rush.

Clemson scored in the second quarter when Terrence Flagler ran 13 yards for a TD. The Tigers drove 80 yards in the third quarter for their second score. Kenny Flowers dove the final yard for the touchdown.

But the Tigers lost two of four fumbles and fell behind, 10-7, at halftime.

Chris Kinzer's 38-yard field goal had given Tech the advantage in the second quarter.

The second lost fumble came when Randy Anderson, who was filling in for Rodney Williams, passed to Flagler, who fumbled at the Tech 13. Hokie defensive tackle Joe Turner recovered the ball and stopped Clemson's scoring threat.

"I don't believe in jinxes," explained Tech coach Bill Dooley. "I told my players that if you get after people, those close games are going to start coming your way."

The Hokies didn't get their first first down by rushing until early in the third quarter. However, quarterback Erik Chapman passed for nine first downs to make up for this.

Chapman passed to tight end Steve Johnson, his favorite receiver, for a 5-yard touchdown pass with 12:06 left in the third quarter to give Tech a 17-7 lead.

Clemson's third-quarter score made it 17-14.

Then in the fourth quarter, Chapman threw a 50-yard pass to split end Don Snell. This set up a 31-yard field goal by Kinzer, which gave the Hokies a 20-14 lead.

Virginia Tech	7	3	7	3	— 20
Clemson	0	7	7	0	— 14

• *Virginia Tech blocked a Clemson punt in the first quarter to score its first touchdown.*

Kinzer Boots Hokies to Peach Bowl Win

ATLANTA, Dec. 31, 1986 — With four seconds left to play, Chris Kinzer preserved his place in Virginia Tech football history by booting a 40-yard field goal to lift the Hokies to a 25-24 win over North Carolina State in the Peach Bowl today.

"I never had any doubt that Chris Kinzer would be successful on the kick at the end," explained Dooley, who coached his final game for the Hokies. "He's the best kicker in college football this year."

It was a near-disastrous offensive holding call, after Tech's Maurice Williams admittedly feigned injury to stop the clock, that Dooley went for the field goal.

The kick, which cleared the goalposts as time expired on the scoreboard clock, completed a wild final 30 minutes. State (8-3-1) saw a 21-10 lead shift to Tech taking the lead, 22-21, then State moving back on top, 24-22, after Mike Cofer's 33-yard field goal. Tech got the ball back with 1:53 to play.

Hokies quarterback Erik Chapman completed four of seven passes on the final drive, including a 5-yarder to tight end Steve Johnson at the State 28 with 15 seconds left.

Tech (9-2-1) was then called for holding with 11 seconds left on the clock, moving the ball back fifteen yards to the State 43.

On the next play, State safety Brian Gay, a third-string substitute, was called for pass interference against Tech wingback David Everett at the goal line.

Two plays later, Kinzer kicked the game-winner — the sixth time he has decided a Tech game this season.

Tech scored first on a 77-yard Peach Bowl-record sprint on the first play of the Hokies' first possession to take a 7-0 lead.

Later in the first quarter, Wolfpack cornerback Derrick Taylor blocked a Tony Romero punt in the end zone. It was recovered by State defensive tackle Brian Bullock to tie the game at 7-7.

Kinzer added a 46-yard field goal with 66 seconds remaining in the quarter to put Tech up, 10-7.

Chapman threw a pair of interceptions before halftime which State converted into touchdowns.

Taylor intercepted the next one on a deep pass from Chapman to Donald Wayne Snell. Six plays later, Kramer threw to Ralph Britt for a 5-yard TD and a 21-10 lead.

In the third quarter, the momentum flipped to the Hokies. Kramer lost a pair of fumbles and Tech converted them into touchdowns.

State got back on top when Cofer booted his 33-yard field goal to put State back in the lead, 24-21.

That set up the ending that kept 53,668 at Atlanta-Fulton County Stadium on the edge of their seats.

Virginia Tech	10	0	6	9 —	25
N.C. State	7	14	0	3 —	24

• *Chris Kinzer's 40-yard field goal with 4 seconds left gave Tech a 25-24 win.*

Hokies Rout Sugar Bowl Bound Cavaliers

BLACKSBURG, Nov. 24, 1990 — The Hokies gift-wrapped a lemon for the Sugar Bowl committee today in front of a Lane Stadium crowd of 54,157, the largest ever to see a game in Virginia.

Tech's 38-13 win over the Sugar Bowl bound, No. 17-ranked Cavaliers is an embarrassment to the New Year's Day matchup with the Southeastern Conference champion.

Virginia, who has now lost three times in their last four games, finished the regular season with an 8-3 record. Earlier in the season, Virginia had been ranked No. 1 in the country for 3 weeks.

Tech's win over the Cavaliers was their first since 1986 and the first in the Frank Beamer era.

The Hokies were helped by Shawn Moore's understudy, Matt Blundin, who completed 21 of 34 passes for 305 yards, but threw three second-half interceptions, fumbled a snap and a handoff with fullback Gary Steele.

A poor punt by the Cavaliers led to the sixth play that led to a total of 17 of Tech's point total.

Will Furrer and Vaughan Hebron combined to make it a long day for Virginia. Furrer completed 16 of 23 passes for 254 yards and 2 TD's. Hebron had 31 carries for 142 yards and one touchdown.

Virginia had allowed opposing teams just 135 yards rushing per game prior to meeting the Hokies.

For bowl-less Tech, who had defeated bowl-bound Southern Miss and North Carolina State, lost to bowl-bound Maryland and Florida State early in the season on late-game plays and lost to No. 3 Georgia Tech on a last-second field goal, they finished the season with a 6-5 record.

"I think we have proved at the end of the season that we are one of the better teams in the country. We deserve to be in a bowl," Beamer noted.

Virginia's offense broke down in the first half and Tech held a 24-6 lead at halftime.

Mark Poindexter ran for 3 yards for Tech's first touchdown in the first quarter. Furrer added another on a 29-yard pass to Nick Cullen.

Mickey Thomas booted a 21-yard field goal in the second quarter and Furrer connected with Greg Daniels on a 33-yard pass for a TD before the half.

In the fourth quarter, Tech added another pair of TD's. Hebron ran for 9 yards with less than 10 minutes to play, then Poindexter grabbed a 3-yard pass from Furrer to wrap up the scoring for Tech.

Virginia's gifted receiver, Herman Moore, caught a 66-yard third-quarter TD pass and finished the afternoon with six catches for 180 yards.

Tech fans celebrated the win over Virginia by tearing down both goalposts.

Virginia	0	6	7	0	— 13
Virginia Tech	14	10	0	14	— 38

• *Vaughn Hebron (4) ran for 131 yards and a fourth-quarter TD.*

Terps' Air Game Grounded

BLACKSBURG, Sept. 25, 1993 — For the third straight week, Maryland quarterback Scott Milanovich set a record for passing yardage, but the Terrapins lost on defense.

Milanovich, while standing outside the visitors' locker room at Lane Stadium in a steady rainfall, explained, "It's frustrating going week in and week out and never able being able to do what we need to do, never getting over the hump, never getting a win." Maryland is now 0-4 for the season.

Tech put together 641 yards of offense this afternoon, including 385 yards rushing.

Maryland managed to outgain the Hokies for a season-high 649 yards. Milanovich completed 29 of 51 passes for 498 yards and 4 TD's, breaking the record of 453 yards he set last week against West Virginia.

Maryland got close early in the fourth quarter. With Tech leading, 41-21, Milanovich threw a 15-yard pass to Walt Williams, who outraced Tech cornerback Larry Green for a 67-yard TD that cut the lead to 41-28.

But Tech struck back with a 57-yard TD pass from Maurice DeShazo to Antonio Freeman.

With 10:41 left to play and a 48-28 lead, DeShazo threw a 40-yard touchdown pass to flanker Jermaine Holmes to complete the scoring at 55-28.

The game's most memorable moment came right

Maurice DeShazo flings a 57-yard touchdown pass to Antonio Freeman. DeShazo finished with 256 yards passing and 3 TD's.

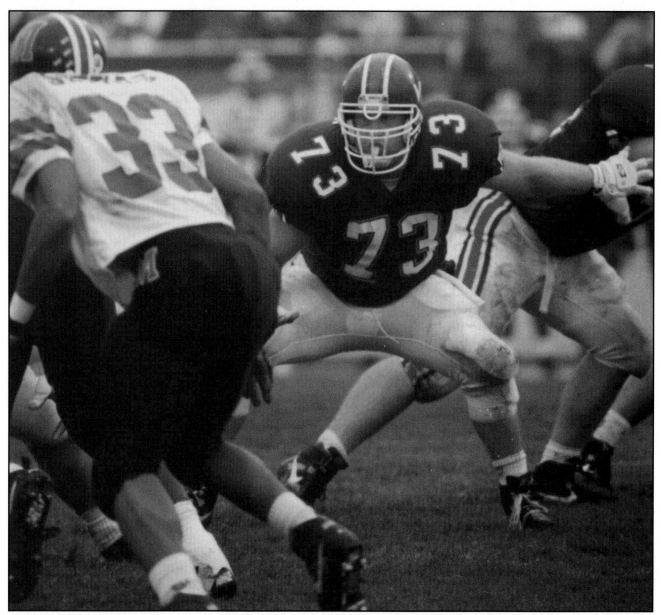

• *Tech's All-American offensive tackle Jim Payne (73) keeps out the Maryland rush.*

before the halftime break.

Trailing 35-14, Maryland had a fourth-and-3 at the Tech 7 and had attempted a 24-yard field goal. But Tech linebacker George DelRicco had burst through and blocked Maryland kicker Ken Lytle's attempt.

The ball then bounced around. Maryland defensive end Sharrod Mack fell on it, but Tech cornerback Tyronne Drakeford kept trying to take it away. This caused the Maryland sideline to get excited and they soon charged the field. Tech's sideline soon charged the field and the scene turned into a brawl. Both coaching staffs soon were on the field, trying to hold back their players while the officials restored order.

It would take seven minutes to send both teams to their locker rooms for intermission.

Maryland	7	7	0	14	—	28
Virginia Tech	7	28	3	17	—	55

• *Dwayne Thomas (42) ran for 93 yards and 1 TD on 18 carries against the Terrapins.*

Hokies Romp Over Hoosiers in Independence Bowl

SHREVEPORT, La., Dec. 31, 1993 — Virginia Tech fans were so excited with the Hokies' 45-20 lead over Indiana in the Independence Bowl that they charged the field with 18 seconds left on the scoreboard clock and danced with the Tech players.

The bowl win — the first for Tech coach Frank Beamer — gave the Hokies a 9-3 record for the 1993 season. The post-game celebration was a long way from Tech's disastrous 2-8-1 season in 1992.

The deciding point in the game occurred in the final 35 seconds before halftime.

The No. 22-ranked Hokies were ahead, 14-13, and were trying to stop the No. 21 Hoosiers, who had a first down at midfield.

Indiana quarterback John Paci was decked by tech linebackers DeWayne Knight and George DelRicco. He fumbled. As Tech tackle J.C. Price tried to recover it, he kicked it toward the Indiana goal line. Tech end Lawrence Lewis picked it on a bounce and ran 20 yards for a touchdown.

Indiana then returned the kickoff 31 yards to the Tech 42. The Hoosiers added eight yards to put the ball at the Tech 34.

The half appeared to be over, but officials put one second back on the clock.

The Hoosiers lined up to attempt a 51-yard field goal. But the attempt was blocked by Jeff Holland and free safety Antonio Banks grabbed the ball in mid-air, turned left and ran 80 yards for a touchdown and give Tech a 28-13 lead.

Tech quarterback Maurice DeShazo, who threw two interceptions today, connected with receiver Antonio Freeman for a 42-yard TD with 9:37 left in the fourth quarter to give Tech a 35-13 lead.

Tech then added another 16 seconds later.

On the Hoosiers' first play after the kickoff, Indiana quarterback Chris Dittoe fumbled after being tackled by Tech defensive lineman Waverly Jackson. Banks recovered the ball and lateraled to Tommy Edwards who scored on a 5-yard run.

Ryan Williams added a 42-yard field goal to wrap up Tech's scoring.

Dittoe then threw a 42-yard pass to Thomas Lewis to pull the Hoosiers to within 45-20.

Indiana scored first on a 75-yard pass from Paci to Lewis to give Indiana a 7-0 lead.

Tech answered with a 73-yard drive, with DeShazo tossing a 13-yard pass to tailback Dwayne Thomas before the first quarter ended.

On Tech's next series, the Hokies scored on a 6-yard run by fullback Joe Swarm to take a 14-7 lead.

The Hoosiers added a pair of 26- and 40-yard field goals to get the score close at 14-13.

Virginia Tech	7	21	0	17	—	45
Indiana	7	6	0	7	—	20

• *Antonio Banks (27) runs 80 yards for a TD after a blocked field-goal attempt before halftime.*

• *Top: Dwayne Thomas (42) scored on a 13-yard pass in the first quarter. Below: J.C. Price chases after Hoosier quarterback Chris Dittoe (11).*

• Top: *Virginia Gov. George Allen celebrates with Frank Beamer in the Tech locker room after the win. Below: Indiana rarely was able to get outside on the Tech defense.*

No. 18 Hokies' Defense Stops Boston College

CHESTNUT HILL, Mass., Sept. 17, 1994 — Undefeated Virgina Tech, the 18th-ranked team in the country pulled off their sixth straight win since last season to defeat Boston College, 12-7, before a crowd of 44,500 at Alumni Field.

Tech won on defense. The Hokies stole four Boston College passes, including one that was returned 66 yards for a touchdown by safety Torrain Gray.

A pair of 48- and 34-yard field goals by Atle Larsen rounded out Tech's scoring.

Boston College's lone score came on a touchdown with six seconds left in the game.

Tech's 3-0 start is their best since 1981.

Virginia Tech committed no turnovers this afternoon after having six last week in a 24-14 win over Southern Mississippi.

"This is a significant win for our program," Tech coach Frank Beamer explained. "I don't think anyone has any concerns about our defense now, and offensively we're very close to getting things done. We're just lucky to be winning while we're looking ragged."

Eagles sophomore quarterback Mark Hartsell, who passed for 338 yards and three touchdowns against No. 4 Michigan two weeks ago, completed only 3 in 11 attempts with two interceptions before being forced to the bench with a hand injury.

A Homecoming crowd at the expanded Alumni Field (12,000 new seats) started booing in the second quarter as each drive began to end in either turnovers or punts.

Hartsell's backups, Jeff Ryan and Scott Mutryn, completed 14 of 36 passes for 160 yards.

Larsen booted his first field goal — a 48-yarder — in the second quarter.

Tech got its only touchdown when a Ryan pass bounced off split end Greg Grice's shoulder pads and into Gray's hands. Gray sprinted into the Boston College end zone for a 9-0 lead.

Tech's extra-point snap failed on bad snap.

Larsen added a 34-yard field goal with 1:08 left in the third quarter.

Boston College's new coach, Dan Henning, a William & Mary alum, explained, "It was a game where if anybody had been able to get something consistently going, they would have had the game to themselves.

"Neither team did, and in our struggle to do so we made the error. That was the ballgame."

Virginia Tech	0	3	9	0 —	12
Boston College	0	0	0	7 —	7

• *Torrain Gray's 66-yard interception return for a touchdown gave Tech a 12-7 win.*

Defense Rules in Rout of West Virginia

BLACKSBURG, Sept. 22, 1994 — Tailback Dwayne Thomas and a strong defense helped No. 14 Virginia Tech overcome a subpar outing by quarterback Maurice Deshazo and take a 34-6 win over slumping West Virginia tonight that was played before a Lane Stadium crowd of 49,679 and an ESPN Thursday night television audience.

Tech is now 4-0 for the first time since 1981.

"It wasn't a real pretty win, but any time you can beat West Virginia you take it," Tech coach Frank Beamer said.

Hokies quarterback Maurice DeShazo completed 12 of 32 passes for 185 yards and two touchdowns, but also had three interceptions.

Thomas rushed 18 times for 94 yards before leaving with a sprained left ankle in the fourth quarter.

Tech (2-0 in the Big East) registered eight sacks on West Virginia quarterbacks, hurried them six other times and intercepted two passes.

West Virginia (1-4, 0-2 in the Big East) is off to its worst start since 1978.

Each of the previous 12 games in the West Virginia-Virginia Tech series has been decided by 12 points or less. But the Mountaineers couldn't keep this one close. West Virginia got no deeper than the Tech 18 in the second half.

DeShazo, a senior who holds several school passing records, came into the game nursing a sprained

ankle and a bruised hip.

West Virginia finished with 239 yards in total offense, with just 91 on the ground.

Tech broke it open by scoring 14 points in a 22-second span midway in the first quarter. Fullback Brian Edmonds put the Hokies ahead to stay when he bulled up the middle on a 33-yard run for a TD, to give Tech a 7-3 lead.

On West Virginia's first play after the kickoff, Eric Broyles' pass was tipped by defensive end Hank Coleman and caught by linebacker Brandon Semones at the Mountaineers' 29.

Two plays later, DeShazo tossed a swing pass to Antonio Freeman and he raced to the West Virginia end zone to give the Hokies a 14-3 lead. Freeman's touchdown catch was the 18th of his career, tying Ricky Scales for the school record.

West Virginia's Bryan Bauman hit a 27-yard field goal to push the score to 14-6.

Ryan Williams then added a pair of 39- and 33-yard field goals in the second quarter to give the Hokies a 20-6 lead.

Bryan Still caught a 35-yard TD pass from DeShazo early in the fourth quarter. Then Ken Oxenride ran for a 53-yard touchdown to wrap up the Hokies' scoring.

West Virginia	3	3	0	0	—	6
Virginia Tech	14	6	0	14	—	34

• *West Virginia backup quarterback Chad Johnston gets sacked by the Tech defense in the fourth quarter.*

Vols Strike Early, Turn Back No. 17 Hokies' Rally

GAINESVILLE, Fla., Dec. 30, 1994 — Turnover-plagued Virginia Tech almost caught up with Tennessee tonight in the Gator Bowl, but it wasn't enough to overcome the Vols' 45-23 lead.

Tech, who had eight turnovers in the regular-season finale against Virginia, fumbled four times, losing one against the Vols.

Hokies quarterback Maurice DeShazo was intercepted twice, leading to a touchdown and a field goal for the Vols.

James Stewart, Tennessee's speedy little tailback, was the deciding factor in the Vols' win. He ran for three touchdowns and threw a 19-yard pass to Kendrick Jones.

Both teams finished the season with 8-4 records, but the unranked Vols won their last five games — scoring 162 points in their last three victories — while the No. 17 Hokies lost three of their last four.

The 68 points scored by the two teams was a Gator Bowl record.

When Dwayne Thomas scored for Tech on a 1-yard run with 5:17 left in the half to reduce Tennessee's lead to 14-7, it ended a string of 148 consecutive points by the Vols, dating back to the second half of their victory over Memphis State in mid-November.

Stewart, the Vols' career rushing leader, scored twice on 1-yard runs and hit Jones on a halfback option pass that gave Tennessee a 35-7 lead with 2:13 left in the half. His final touchdown — a 4-yard run early in the fourth quarter — gave the Volunteers a 42-16 lead.

Peyton Manning, the son of former Ole Miss and NFL great Archie Manning, led the Vols to seven victories in their last eight games after taking over as the starting quarterback following season-ending injuries to Jerry Colquitt and Todd Helton.

He led Tennessee to a 21-0 lead in the first 17 minutes of the game.

The Vols capitalized on a Tech turnover 15 seconds into the game for their first score. Linebacker Tyrone Hines picked off a DeShazo pass at the Tech 27. Eight plays later, Stewart's 1-yard TD run put the Vols on the scoreboard with a 7-0 lead.

Manning, the SEC freshman of the year, who completed six of his first seven passes for 123 yards and a touchdown, lobbed a 36-yard TD pass to Marcus Nash to climax a 93-yard drive to put the Vols up, 14-0.

On the next drive, Jones went 76 yards on a flanker reverse following a crushing reverse by Kevin Mays to set up a 1-yard touchdown run by Jay Graham and a 21-0 Vols' lead.

Freshman quarterback Branndon Stewart replaced Manning late in the first half and led the Vols to two more touchdowns.

○ *Maurice DeShazo scrambles 8 yards for a third-quarter touchdown.*

DeShazo, Tech's career leader in total offense and touchdown passes, scored on a third-quarter, 8-yard scramble to make it 35-16. But Ryan Williams missed the extra-point kick.

Bryan Still caught a 9-yard touchdown pass from Tech backup quarterback Jim Druckenmiller with four minutes left in the game to narrow the score to 45-23.

Ryan Williams kicked a 28-yard field goal in the second quarter for Tech's other score.

• Freshman quarterback Peyton Manning (16) passed for 189 yards and 1 touchdown.

Virginia Tech	0	10	6	7	—	23
Tennessee	14	21	0	10	—	45

Tech Finally Ends Streak to Feisty Hurricanes

BLACKSBURG, Sept. 23, 1995 — Virginia Tech, winless in its first two games of the season, had never beaten the Miami Hurricanes in 13 previous attempts since 1953. But today, before a sellout crowd of 51,206 at Lane Stadium, Tech finally defeated the No. 17 Hurricanes, 13-7, and a wild celebration followed.

Both goalposts eventually came down.

Miami hadn't lost to an unranked team in 71 games prior to today.

It was the Hurricanes' second loss in the Big East Conference since joining the conference more than two seasons ago. West Virginia defeated the Hurricanes, 17-14, on Nov. 20, 1993.

The Hokies (1-2, 1-0 in the Big East) had six sacks, six tackles behind the line of scrimmage and held Miami (1-2, 0-1 in the Big East) to 51 yards rushing — its worst performance since gaining only two yards rushing against Arizona in 1992.

Still, Miami had the opportunity to pull out a win. After getting the ball at its 25 and slighty more than two minutes left, backup quarterback Ryan Clement and Yatil Green combined for 4 completions and 39 yards to move the Hurricanes from the Tech 10 to midfield with 46 seconds remaining.

Then on the next play, Tech defensive tackle J.C. Price sacked Clement for a 10-yard loss. Clement's next two passes fell incomplete.

Druckenmiller completed 9 of 16 passes for only 97 yards, but the Tech offense put together a total of 397 yards in total offense. Tech's 300 yards in rushing kept the ball away from Miami's aerial attack.

Last season, the Hokies lost 14 yards rushing against Miami.

"We knew from the first drive down the field we had this game," said tailback Dwayne Thomas, who ran for 165 yards.

"Coach said, 'We're going to run it down their throats,' and that's exactly what we did. Our line was opening holes big enough for a Mack truck to go through."

The Hokies ran the ball nine straight times on the first series of the game to reach the Miami 8. Atle Larsen's field goal attempt was blocked.

The next time Tech got the ball, Druckenmiller connected with Bryan Still on a 47-yard pass to move the ball to the Miami 1-yard line. Thomas dove over the middle for the touchdown to give Tech a 7-0 lead with 3:09 left in the first quarter.

Miami didn't get the ball moving until the second quarter. Ryan Collins completed passes of 47 and 11 yards before throwing an interception to Brandon Sermones at the Tech 8.

Ken Oxenride carried the ball on seven of 12 plays on Tech's next drive. When the Hokies got stuck at the Miami 27, Larsen booted a 44-yarder to give the Hokies a 10-0 lead.

• *Dwayne Thomas (42), who ran for 165 yards and 1 TD, races through the Miami secondary.*

Danyell Ferguson scored the Hurricanes' only touchdown in the second quarter to tighten the score to 10-7.

Larsen booted a 20-yard field goal in the fourth quarter to wrap up the scoring at 13-7.

Collins suffered a sprained shoulder while being tackled with 3:55 left in the first half by Tech free safety William Yarborough.

• *Dwayne Thomas (42) dives for a 1-yard TD in the first quarter.*

	1	2	3	4		
Miami	0	7	0	0	—	7
Virginia Tech	7	3	0	3	—	13

Banks' Last-Minute Steal Seals Cavs' Fate

CHARLOTTESVILLE, Nov. 18, 1995 — Virginia drove downfield in the final minute today in an attempt to either score a touchdown or a field goal to overcome Tech's 30-29 lead.

But Hokie cornerback Antonio Banks intercepted a Mike Groh pass and ran it 65 yards for a touchdown on the game's final play to dash the Cavaliers' hopes and give Tech a 36-29 win in the 100th anniversary of this storied rivalry.

43,600 at Scott Stadium had been on the edge of their seats in the game's final moments. Finally, Tech fans were able to celebrate the end of a 9-2 regular season and the possible invitation to the Sugar Bowl on New Year's Eve.

Virginia, who had grabbed a share of the ACC championship, led by 15 points going into the final quarter but couldn't hold on.

The Cavaliers finished with an 8-4 record. Two of Virginia's losses were to Michigan and Texas.

Tech took a 30-29 lead with 47 seconds remaining after driving 71 yards for a touchdown. Hokies' receiver Jermaine Holmes snagged a 32-yard pass from Jim Druckenmiller in the Virginia end zone for the score.

The Cavaliers scored first in the contest after Adrian Burnim and Stephen Plalan blocked a Tech punt. Virginia then traveled 33 yards in three plays. Germane Crowell caught a 29-yard Groh pass in the end zone for the score and a 7-0 lead.

The Hokies then scored twice to jump ahead, 14-7.

Backup quarterback Tim Sherman then drove the Cavaliers 70 yards for a touchdown. Sherman's 2-point pass gave Virginia a 15-14 lead.

Groh later returned after being treated in the locker room, but Sherman stayed on the field at quarterback.

He then led Virginia to another touchdown before halftime. The 67-yard drive gave the Cavaliers a 22-14 lead. Crowell pulled in Sherman's 31-yard TD pass for the score.

Virginia added to its lead on its first possession of the third quarter. The Cavaliers drove 74 yards, with Tiki Barber scoring on a 9-yard run to give Virginia a 29-14 lead.

Tech then got moving in the fourth quarter.

Holmes scored on a 10-yard run and Larsen booted a field goal to get Tech close at 29-23.

Afterward, the Hokies' final two touchdowns in the last minute put Tech on top.

Virginia Tech	14	0	0	22	—	36
Virginia	7	15	7	0	—	29

Jim Druckenmiller (16), who passed for 230 yards and 2 TD's, searches for a receiver downfield.

• *Tech took a 30-29 lead in the last minute. Afterward, Tech fans flooded the field, tearing down the goalposts.*

• *Atle Larsen and his holder, John Thomas (3), celebrate after taking a 30-29 lead in the final minute.*

Tech Romps Over No. 9 Longhorns in Sugar Bowl

NEW ORLEANS, Dec. 31, 1995 — In the quiet of the night on New Year's Eve, after the Sugar Bowl had been played, Virginia Tech coach Frank Beamer was smiling, looking back at the 1995 season and wondering if it could get any better.

With Bryan Still returning a punt for one touchdown and catching a 54-yard pass for another, Beamer's Hokies concluded the greatest season in Virginia Tech history by pounding the Texas Longhorns, 28-10, in the Sugar Bowl.

It was the 10th straight win for the No. 13 Hokies (10-2), who were co-champions of the Big East with Miami, and could give them their first-ever Top 10 finish.

Still and the Hokies' punishing defense, which blitzed Texas into submission, were the two key reasons Tech got its first major bowl win.

Still also set up the Hokies' second touchdown with one of his six catches and was named the game's most valuable player.

But for nearly two quarters, the Sugar Bowl officials must have looked at the Hokies and surely wondered, "How did we pick these turkeys?"

Virginia Tech looked as nervous and miscast as the last Big East team to play here (West Virginia, a 41-7 loser to Florida two years ago).

No. 9 Texas (10-2-1), who entered the game with a 21-0-1 record under UT coach John Mackovic

while leading at halftime, led by 10-7 at intermission.

But the Hokies, who sacked quarterback James Brown five times and forced him into three interceptions, were to take control in the second half.

The momentum actually began to change dramatically for the Hokies when Still returned a punt 60 yards for a TD with 2 minutes 34 seconds left in the first half. With Tech leading, 14-10, he caught a 54-yard touchdown pass from Jim Druckenmiller, and the Hokies were ahead for good.

Tech trailed at halftime despite limiting Texas to just 126 yards in total offense. The Hokies, 10th in the nation in total defense, No. 5 in scoring defense and No. 1 against the rush, held Texas to just 226 yards.

Shon Mitchell, who rushed for 1,099 yards last season, managed to get only 57 on 11 carries tonight. Freshman Ricky Williams, who gained 990 yards this year, had 62 on 12 carries.

Tech scored its final touchdown with 5:06 left when Cornell Brown picked up his second sack of the game, causing a fumble by James Brown that Jim Baron returned 20 yards. Brown later added another sack, giving Tech 49 for the season.

Baron's touchdown was the seventh defensive score in the last six games for the Hokies.

Texas scored first, taking a 7-0 lead with 4:32 left in the first quarter. After gaining just one first down on its first two possessions, Texas went 72 yards.

Tech took its first lead with 2:32 left in the third

• *Bryan Still caught a 54-yard TD pass and returned a punt 60 yards for another touchdown.*

quarter, when Marcus Parker capped a 67-yard drive with a 2-yard touchdown run. The Hokies went on top, 14-10.

For Beamer and the Hokies it was a great way to begin the New Year.

"We've got a lot riding on this thing," said the Virginia Tech coach. His Hokies, having won their first Big East title, were playing in the school's first major bowl.

"It gives us an opportunity to take another step," said Beamer. "Texas is at the point where we're trying to get to. They have the national reputation, been to many bowls, won their conference many times. We're trying to get there and I think we have the potential to.

"If we can find a way to beat Texas, it makes us more legit. And I think (it would prove) these fine people at the Sugar Bowl didn't make a mistake in inviting Virginia Tech."

• *Marcus Parker (34) runs two yards for a TD in the third quarter to cap a 67-yard drive.*

Virginia Tech	0	7	7	14	—	28
Texas	7	3	0	0	—	10

No. 21 Hokies Rally to Defeat No. 18 Hurricanes

MIAMI, Nov. 16, 1996 — Frank Beamer's Virginia Tech Hokies defeated Miami, 21-7, at the Orange Bowl for the first time in school history this evening.

They had to overcome a stirring 40-mph wind that turned the aging stadium into a wind tunnel.

The game broke open late in third quarter when Tech quarterback Jim Druckenmiller tossed a 13-yard pass to wide receiver Michael Stuewe. Then in the game's final three minutes safety Keion Carpenter's 100-yard interception return for a touchdown clinched the victory.

It was the Hokies' second straight win over the No. 18 Hurricanes. Last season, Tech defeated Miami, 13-7, in Blacksburg — their first ever victory over the Hurricanes.

"It's a dream come true to come here and beat Miami," said Druckenmiller, who completed 15 of 24 passes for 202 yards and no interceptions. "We've had so many big wins, it's hard to pick just one that stands out. This one is certainly up there with any of them. We had a game to play, regardless of the surroundings. Good teams block out what's around them and play football."

Tech entered the game with an all-time record of 1-12 against Miami.

Earlier this season, the Hurricanes set an NCAA record for consecutive home victories, defeating Georgia Southern for their 56th straight win.

Recently, however, Miami has had problems winning at home. The Hurricanes won their first two home games, then lost to Florida State and East Carolina — and, now, Tech.

Miami hasn't lost three home games in a season since 1984 during Jimmy Johnson's first year as head coach.

Tech drove 86 yards in 12 plays on its first possession of the game. Ken Oxenride dove one yard on fourth-and-goal for the TD and take a 7-0 lead.

The Hurricanes were flagged for an illegal block on the ensuing kickoff, pushing the ball back to the Miami 8.

Miami then marched 92 yards in 12 plays, with Ryan Clement passing two yards to Chris Jones in the end zone.

With only three seconds left before halftime, Tech stopped a Miami drive inside the Hokies' 1.

In the Hokies' first drive of the third quarter, they drove to the Miami 38, which was set up by Oxenride's two runs totaling 28 yards. The drive ended when Oxenride lost a yard on a carry and Druckenmiller an incomplete pass to Brian Edmonds.

Tech later regained the lead in the third quarter when Druckenmiller threw a 13-yard pass to Stuewe in the end zone to put the Hokies up, 14-7.

• *Jim Druckenmiller (16), who threw for 202 yards, passes to Michael Steuwe for a 13-yard TD.*

Carpenter's 100-yard interception return for a touchdown in the fourth quarter wrapped up the scoring.

Druckenmiller was productive in the first half, completing 9 of 12 passes for 137 yards.

Oxenride lead all ballcarriers, with for 89 yards on 19 carries.

• *Above: Keion Carpenter's 100-yard interception return for a TD in the final three minutes sealed Tech's win. Right: Cornell Brown (58) puts pressure on Miami quarterback Ryan Clement.*

Virginia Tech	7	0	7	7	—	21
Miami	7	0	0	0	—	7

Cornhuskers Roar in Second Half to Defeat Tech

MIAMI, Dec. 31, 1996 — The Nebraska Cornhuskers' two-year national championship reign ends this week, but they went out in style tonight in the Orange Bowl with a 41-21 win over Big East co-champion, the Hokies of Virginia Tech.

Nebraska defensive tackle Jason Peter scored on a 31-yard fumble return and the Cornhuskers lit up the scoreboard with touchdowns on each of its first four possessions in the third quarter to ensure the win.

The game was the first Orange Bowl played in December and the first held at the new Pro Player Stadium. The crowd of 51,212 was the smallest in fifty years.

No. 6 Nebraska (11-2) earned its third consecutive bowl victory and reached 11 victories for the fourth year in the row. The Cornhuskers' bid for an unprecedented third straight national title ended with an upset loss to Texas in the Big 12 championship game.

No. 10 Virginia Tech (10-2) lost despite Jim Druckenmiller's three touchdown passes and Ken Oxendine's 210-yard rushing effort. Oxendine ran for 150 yards in 20 carries and added 60 yards on three receptions.

Oxendine was voted the Hokies' most valuable player. Damon Benning, the Cornhuskers' MVP, rushed for 95 yards and scored on runs of 33 and 6 yards.

Nebraska, a 17-point favorite, struck for 17 points in a 10-minute span in the second quarter, including one score by the defense when Tech tried to run the option on third-and-37.

Druckenmiller was about to pitch on the play when he was hit by Nebraska's Mike Rucker, and the ball squirted free. The 285-pound Peter picked it up and ran 31 yards untouched for the touchdown.

Nebraska led by 17-14 at halftime, then cranked out scoring drives of 74, 61, 76 and 55 yards in its first four possessions of the second half.

Quarterback Scott Frost scored on runs of 5 and 22 yards, and Kris Brown kicked field goals of 25 and 37 yards for the Cornhuskers, who snapped Tech's seven-game winning streak.

The Hokies closed to within 17-14 at halftime by driving 80 yards in the final 3:36 of the first half. Tech scored with 19 seconds left before intermission on Druckenmiller's 6-yard pass to Shawn Scales.

Druckenmiller also threw a 19-yard touchdown pass to Marcus Parker and a 33-yarder to Cornelius White. The Hokies' quarterback completed 16 of 33 passes for 214 yards.

Virginia Tech	7	7	7	0	— 21
Nebraska	0	17	14	10	— 41

● *Jim Druckenmiller (16) completed 16 of 33 passes for 214 yards and 3 TD's, but it wasn't enough to keep up with Nebraska.*

• *Cornelius White pulls in a pass 33-yard third-quarter pass from Jim Druckenmiller.*

• *Shawn Scales fights for a 6-yard TD pass.*

Prioleau's' 2-Point Interception Stops Hurricanes

BLACKSBURG, Nov. 8, 1997 — Virginia Tech and Miami battled to the end with one spectacular play after another, but in the end a combination of defense and special teams made the difference in the No. 20 Hokies' 27-25 win tonight.

With less than 2 minutes to play, Tech's Pierson Prioleau intercepted a 2-point pass that would have tied the game.

Miami was successful on the on-side kick that followed, but a penalty nullified the play, giving the ball to the Hokies, who held on for their third straight victory over the Hurricanes, who won the first 12 meetings between the two teams.

If Tech (7-2, 5-1 in the Big East) defeats Pitt in their next game, they will claim a share of their third consecutive Big East championship and a possible third straight Alliance Bowl berth.

"We're taking these things in stages. One more win and we're Big East champions. We need to keep playing hard and keep winning and things will take care of themselves," Tech coach Frank Beamer said.

The Hokies rushed for 259 yards tonight. Senior tailback Ken Oxenride led the ground attack with 147 yards on 36 carries.

The game got close after Shayne Graham booted a 22-yard field goal with 3:58 left to play, which gave Tech a 27-19 lead.

The Hurricanes (4-5, 2-3 in the Big East) then drove 66 yards on six plays for a touchdown. Tailback James Jackson scored on a 12-yard run to close Tech's lead to 27-25.

Jackson ran for 142 yards on just nine carries.

Miami already had an extra-point kick blocked and a 2-point pass ruled out of bounds earlier in the fourth quarter.

"It's every little boy's dream to be a hero for his team," Prioleau explained. "I was in the right place at the right time to make a great play for the team down to the wire."

Backup fullback Cullen Hawkins scored his first career touchdown to give Tech a 17-13 lead in the third quarter on a 14-yard run up the middle.

Tech's defense began to come to life late in the third quarter when they stopped the Hurricanes at the Tech 40 by sacking the quarterback twice and forcing a punt.

"We got the crowd on our side after that," said Hokies cornerback Loren Johnson. "I think that was the turning point of the game."

Hokies reserve tailback Lamont Pegues scored seven plays later on a 27-yard run to give Tech a 24-13 lead as the third quarter ended.

Al Clark, the Hokies' quarterback, completed 10 of 12 passes for 153 yards tonight.

"I think he made a couple third-down plays that were fantastic," Beamer said of Clark.

The Hurricanes made it close again with a 78-

Al Clark (5), who completed 10 of 12 passes for
153 yards, outruns the Miami defense.

yard TD run by Jackson with 10:59 left to play. Ryan Clement's 2-point play to Wayne in the corner of the end zone was ruled out of bounds.

Clement scored first for Miami with a 6-yard touchdown run in the first quarter. James added another on a 4-yard run before the quarter was over.

Graham kicked a 22-yard field goal in the first quarter and Marcus Parker scored on a 7-yard run to wrap up Tech's first-half scoring.

• *Top: Marcus Parker (34) rips for a 7-yard TD in the second quarter. Right: Ike Charlton (3) reaches for a pass in the Miami end zone.*

Miami	13	0	0	12	—	25
Virginia Tech	3	7	14	3	—	27

Clark's Overtime TD Pass Defeats Hurricanes

MIAMI, Sept. 19, 1998 — Turnovers by their opponent and Al Clark's touchdown pass to Ricky Hall were the difference tonight as Virginia Tech defeated Miami, 27-20, in overtime, giving the Hokies their fourth straight win over the Hurricanes.

Miami's fatal blow came when they committed turnovers on five straight possessions in the second and third quarters.

The Hokies had an opportunity to win the game outright, but Shayne Graham missed a 36-yard field goal attempt with 12 seconds left to play.

Tech then got the ball first in overtime. On the second play, Clark threw a pass to Hall, the Hokies' 6-3, 207 lb. wide receiver, who outjumped the Hurricanes' 5-10 cornerback, Nick Ward, in the end zone for the touchdown.

During Miami's turn, quarterback Scott Covington was sacked twice. Then on fourth down from the 32, he threw an incomplete pass.

"I just knew we had to come out and make a big play," Hall said. "I was hoping we'd have enough stamina and poise on the line so we could end this game."

The win was special for the Hokies (3-0, 1-0 in the Big East), but the loss left Miami coach Butch Davis 0-4 against Tech.

"They were the better team," Davis said. "I was disappointed with how we played. We self-destructed out there tonight."

Shyrone Stith led the Hokies' rushing attack with 63 yards on 16 carries. Tech had 272 total yards on the ground.

Clark completed 14 of 26 passes for 153 yards, one interception and 2 TD's.

Miami (2-1, 0-1 in the Big East), who wore green jerseys for the first time since 1976, got 96 yards rushing from halfback Edgerrin James. Covington added 282 yards passing and three TDs, with 13 completions on 28 attempts. He also had one interception.

Miami was ahead, 13-3, when Covington fumbled and Tech defensive end Chris Cyrus recovered at the Hurricanes' 26. A few plays later, Clark hit Cullen Hawkins on a 14-yard touchdown pass to pull the score up to 13-10.

Late in the third quarter, Miami's fourth turnover — another fumble by Covington — set up a 13-yard TD by Clark to put Tech in the lead, 17-13.

Miami went back ahead with 14:45 left in the game on an 84-yard touchdown play. Covington threw a high pass that Hurricanes receivers Santana Moss and Reggie Wayne leaped high with Tech defender Ike Charlton to get the pass. Wayne came down with the ball and raced for the Hokies' end zone and a 20-17 lead.

Graham tied the game up six minutes later with a

• *Hokie receiver Ricky Hall (82) reaches high for a 24-yard TD pass from Al Clark to win the game in overtime.*

• Above: Tech tailback Shyrone Stith (38) rumbled for 63 yards on 16 carries against Miami. Right: Lamont Pegues (7), who ran for 22 yards on 4 carries, sprints on a draw play.

19-yard field goal.

Miami jumped out to a 7-0 lead when Covington flung a 47-yard touchdown pass to Moss with 5:54 left in the first quarter.

Graham got his first field goal in the second quarter to make it 7-3 after a 38-yard kick that capped a 13-play, 58-yard drive.

On Miami's next series, the Hurricanes marched 73 yards in 12 plays for a TD. Covington passed 15 yards to Wayne for the score. Tech blocked the extra-point attempt, leaving Miami with a 13-3 lead.

Miami's turnovers began two minutes later.

Virginia Tech	0	10	7	3	7	— 27
Miami	7	6	0	7	0	— 20

Hokies' Defense Dominates Tide in Music City Bowl

NASHVILLE, Dec. 29, 1998 — It took the Virginia Tech Hokies 10 tries, but they finally put an end to a losing streak that began in 1932 with a 38-7 rout of Alabama in the inaugural Music City Bowl.

The one-sided victory put an end to a two-game bowl losing streak for Tech and buried many demons from yesteryear. The Hokies are one of only 10 teams who have been to bowl games each of the last six years. The win was also Tech's first win over a Southeastern Conference team in this decade.

Tech's defense and special teams was dominating tonight, with six turnovers — three interceptions, two blocked punts, and recovering a muffed punt.

For Alabama (7-5), with second-year coach Mike DuBose, it was his first bowl appearance and the end of a five-game winning streak. It was also the Tide's worst loss in a bowl game since losing to national champion Nebraska, 38-6, in the 1972 Orange Bowl.

"They're a team that's at a level that we're trying to get to," said DuBose, who is trying to rebuild the program to the level it had under Bear Bryant and Gene Stallings.

Tech (9-3) blew open a close game in the third quarter with the great defensive play of MVP Corey Moore.

Moore's fierce rush from the left side forced Alabama quarterback Andrew Zow to throw an inter-ception from the Tide 6 in the third quarter and the Hokies scored after the turnover to take a 17-7 lead.

Later in the third quarter, Moore ran through the middle of Alabama's protection and blocked a punt, which led to another Virginia Tech touchdown. Tech's lead was now 24-7.

A crowd of 41,600 at Vanderbilt Stadium saw the game quickly turn into a rout.

"This is what people are going to remember, this bowl win," Moore said. "We've thought about how close we were to an undefeated season. This makes up for some of that."

Tech lost three games by a total of 10 points in the regular season.

In the first half, it appeared Tech might botch the game just as it did in botching losses to Temple, Syracuse and Virginia.

The Hokies led, 10-7, but they failed to capitalize on a blocked punt and an interception. In addition, Tech quarterback Al Clark missed on a pass to a wide-open Shyrone Stith inside the Alabama 10-yard line in the second quarter.

"There was concern, sure, you start worrying about how many of those you're going to get," Tech coach Frank Beamer said. "Fortunately, we got some more."

Those opportunities came in bunches in the second half as wind chill took temperatures down to 14 degrees. The Hokies' pass rush quickly heated up and

*Al Clark's 43-yard TD run in the first quarter set
the stage for Tech's rout over Alabama.*

• *Tech's special teams blocked 2 Alabama punts and recovered a muffed punt during the Music City Bowl.*

started to run down Zow, forcing the redshirt fresh-man to make crucial mistakes.

From his 6-yard line, he tried to throw over the middle, but his arm was hit by Moore. Tech line-backer Phillip Summers intercepted it.

Lamont Pegues scored two plays later from the Tide 1. Shayne Graham's extra-point kick made it 17-7.

On Alabama's next possession, Moore was back at work. He raced through the middle and blocked Daniel Pope's punt. Summers recovered it at the Tide 29.

"We were getting a jump on the the snap," Moore explained. "That's why we were blocking the punts."

A questionable pass interference gave Tech the ball at the Tide 4. Stith powered over from the left side for the TD. Graham's extra-point kick gave Tech

a 24-7 lead with 5 minutes 8 seconds left in the third quarter.

Tech's defense held Shaun Alexander, the SEC's third-leading rusher, to just 55 yards on 21 carries — 37 of these yards came in the fourth quarter with the game out of reach.

Tech's offense played only well enough to win. The Hokies had only 207 rushing yards and 71 in passing.

"The defense and special teams gave us the turnovers," Clark explained. "Then we put it in the end zone."

Virginia Tech	7	3	14	14	— 28
Alabama	0	7	0	0	— 7

• *Music City Bowl MVP Corey Moore (56) spent a lot of time in the Alabama backfield.*

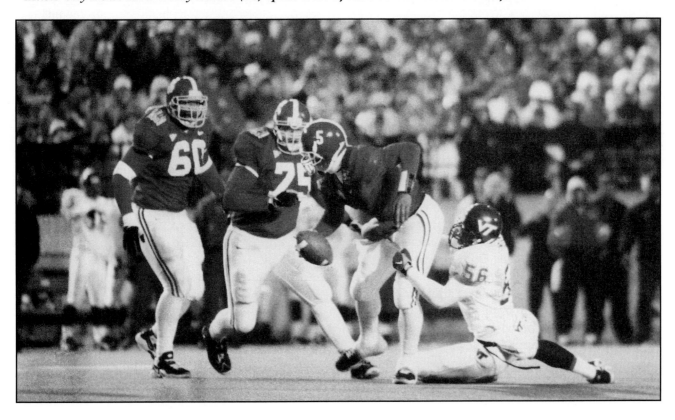

No. 4 Hokies Revenge Loss to Syracuse

BLACKSBURG, Oct. 16, 1999 — And who says payback doesn't feel good?

The No. 4-ranked Hokies, who had to live with the sickening feeling of last year's last-second loss to Syracuse in the Carrier Dome, made up for it by routing the No. 16 Orangemen, 62-0.

The game began as a battle for first place in the Big East. But Tech's Shyrone Stith, who ran for 140 yards and a pair of touchdowns, and Michael Vick, who threw for a TD and field-generaled the Hokies to victory, quickly changed that. Lane Stadium has rarely seen such a blowout.

The margin of victory was the largest for Virginia Tech since a 73-0 triumph over Catholic University in 1922. It was also Syracuse's worst defeat since a 62-0 drubbing by Princeton in 1912.

The Hokies (6-0, 2-0 in the Big East) also scored two defensive touchdowns and one on special teams.

Syracuse (5-2, 2-1 in the Big East) won last year's meeting on a last-second touchdown pass by Donovan McNabb, coming from behind after trailing, 21-3, to post a 28-26 win.

This year, Virginia Tech never trailed and dominated the Orangemen from the start. The Hokies rolled up 411 yards on offense and held Syracuse to just 120 yards and seven first downs.

The Virginia Tech defense forced a three-and-out on Syracuse's first possession of the game and the Hokie special teams appeared to score on a punt return for a touchdown, but an illegal block penalty brought the ball back to the Tech 25-yard line. Virginia Tech was stopped on its first possession, but rolled from there.

The Orangemen took over after a punt, but the Hokie defense got the scoring started. Quinton Spotwood caught a pass near the left sideline, but fumbled and Cory Bird scooped up the loose ball and raced 26 yards for a touchdown and a 7-0 lead.

Stith ran one yard for a touchdown and a 14-0 lead with 2:24 left in the first quarter and Vick hit Ricky Hall with an eight-yard touchdown pass just over two minutes into the second quarter to make it 21-0.

Stith scored on a one-yard run with 6:13 to play in the second quarter to increase Tech's lead to 28-0. Shayne Graham added a 25-yard field goal just 23 seconds before the half to boost that cushion to 31-0.

The Hokies outgained the Orangemen 229-34 in the first half and limited Syracuse to just one first down.

Virginia Tech continued to pour it on in the second half, as Stith ran 58 yards on the first play from scrimmage to set up a 37-yard field goal by Graham.

Syracuse punter Mike Shafer mishandled a snap after the next possession for the Orangemen and was tackled at the Virginia Tech 10-yard line. The Hokies quickly added another touchdown, as Andre

Hokie freshman quarterback Michael Vick (7) completed 8 of 16 passes for 135 yards and 1 TD.

Kendrick took a pitch from Vick on an option play and raced seven yards for a score and a 41-0 lead with 10:08 left in the third quarter.

Andre Davis added a 28-yard touchdown on a reverse with 1:31 left in the third for a 48-0 advantage. Phillip Summers later returned an interception 43 yards for a touchdown with 4:56 left.

Tee Butler wrapped up Tech's scoring spree by recovering a fumble in the end zone on another bad punt snap with 2:33 remaining to push the Hokies' total to 62-0.

• Shyrone Stith (38) ran for 140 yards on 22 carries and 2 TD's.

Syracuse	0	0	0	0	—	0
Virginia Tech	14	17	17	14	—	62

Graham's Last-Second Kick Defeats WVa.

MORGANTOWN, W.Va., Nov. 6, 1999 — It was the game-winning kick that Virginia Tech kicker Shayne Graham had long dreamed of.

When given the opportunity, Graham stepped up and delivered a 44-yard field goal as time expired to give the No. 3-ranked Hokies a 22-20 win and another unforgettable memory in this magical season.

The Hokies (8-0, 4-0 in the Big East) struggled the entire game against a 19-point underdog.

West Virginia (3-6, 2-3 in the Big East) was left out of the bowl picture for the first time since 1995.

Coupled with Minnesota's 24-23 upset of No. 2 Penn State, Tech's lackluster victory could throw the Bowl Championship Series standings into a free-for-all. The standings determine which teams will meet for the national championship matchup in the Sugar Bowl on Jan. 4.

Virginia Tech appeared to have the game in hand after Shyrone Stith scored on a 6-yard run with five minutes left for a 19-7 lead.

Backup Mountaineer quarterback Brad Lewis, who took over after Marc Bulger hurt his thumb and sat out the second half, threw two TD passes in the final three minutes to put WVa ahead, 20-19.

The Hokies got the ball back at their 16 and freshman Michael Vick marched his team 58 yards in seven plays to set up the winning kick.

The game marked the first time this season that Virginia Tech, the nation's third-best scoring offense, was held under 30 points.

After Stith's touchdown, West Virginia's Richard Bryant fumbled the ensuing kickoff at his 14. Mountaineer Boo Sensabaugh quickly scooped up the ball and returned it down the right sideline for 47 yards to the Tech 39. A late-hit penalty on the play moved the ball to the Tech 24.

Seven plays later, Lewis hit Jerry Porter from four yards to cut the deficit to 19-14 with 3:15 left.

On Tech's next possession, Stith fumbled and Sensabaugh recovered at the Tech 32 with 1:46 left. On third-and-13 at the 18, Lewis hit Khori Ivy in the end zone for a 20-19 lead.

The game produced several firsts for Tech.

Virginia Tech was held scoreless in the first quarter for the first time this season.

West Virginia redshirt freshman Avon Cobourne rushed for 133 yards, the most allowed by the nation's top rushing defense this season.

Vick finished 14 completions on 30 attempts for 255 yards. Lewis went 9 of 16 for 98 yards.

Stith, the Big East's top rusher, was held to 84 yards — 28 below his average.

Virginia Tech	0	7	5	10	— 22
West Virginia	0	7	0	13	— 20

126

Shayne Graham (17) was the hero of the game with his 44-yard field goal as time ran out.

• *Michael Vick completed 14 of 30 attempts for 255 yards against West Virginia.*

• *Andre Davis (88) hauled in five passes for 138 yards — a 27.6 yards per catch average.*

Dreaming of Sugar, No. 2 Tech Routs Hurricanes

BLACKSBURG, Nov. 13, 1999 — Four years after what Virginia Tech fans consider the school's breakthrough victory, the Hokies faithful can celebrate the biggest win in the program's history.

Behind a suffocating defense and an heroic effort from freshman redshirt quarterback Michael Vick, the No. 2 Hokies proved their worth to the nation by crushing Big East Conference rival and No. 19 Miami, 43-10, in front of a raucous Lane Stadium crowd of 53,130.

With Tennessee's loss earlier in the day, Virginia Tech will almost certainly move back to second in the Bowl Championship Series ratings, which determines the participants for the Sugar Bowl, where the national title will be decided on January 4, 2000.

The Hokies forced six turnovers and battered Miami quarterback Kenny Kelly, eventually knocking him from the game in the third quarter with a twisted left ankle. Anthony Midget intercepted three passes and fellow cornerback Ike Charlton returned a fumble 51 yards for a touchdown.

Virginia Tech (9-0, 5-0 in the Big East) scored 43 unanswered points after falling behind 10-0 in the first 10 ½ minutes and defeated the Hurricanes (5-4, 3-1 in the Big East) for the fifth straight season after losing their first 12 to them.

It was a 13-7 home win over Miami in 1995 that put the Hokies on the national stage and allowed them to capture their first Big East title en route to a Sugar Bowl victory over Texas. Another league title and an Orange Bowl appearance followed the next season.

The last two meetings between the schools had been decided by a total of nine points, but the Hokies were out to prove a point — that they belong in the Sugar Bowl despite a schedule ranked 60th in the nation.

Playing with a bad left ankle that has bothered him most of the season, Vick completed 11 of 23 passes for 151 yards and carried 14 times for 46 yards, leading the Hokies to their first 9-0 start.

Miami scored first with a 28-yard field goal by Andy Crossland. It was the first time all season that a Tech opponent had scored first.

Miami made it 10-0 after a 49-yard drive that ended in a 7-yard pass from Kelly to Eric King.

It was a slide downhill for the Hurricanes from there.

Charlton recovered a Clinton Portis fumble and returned it 11 yards. Miami was then hit with a 12-yard personal foul penalty after the play that put the ball at the Miami 12.

Andre Kendrick swept left to take the ball to the Miami 1. Four plays later, Shrone Stith banged over for the TD. Graham's extra-point kick made it 10-7.

Miami tight end Daniel Franks (88) can't escape from Hokie defender Ike Charlton.

The Hurricanes' third of four turnovers in the first half led to Tech's go-ahead score. Midget stepped in front of a pass intended for Santana Moss at the Miami 42 to give Tech the ball.

Two plays later, Stith ripped through a big hole in the middle of the line and raced 41 yards for the touchdown to take a 14-10 lead.

Shayne Graham added a pair of field goals in the third quarter to up Tech's lead to 20-10.

Ricky Hall's 64-yard punt return for a TD — the Hokies' first since Bryan Still's 1995 Sugar Bowl run — made it 27-10.

Charlton scooped up a fumble and ran 51 yards for a touchdown that gave Tech a 33-10 lead with 13:39 left to play.

Graham booted his third field goal — this one for 45 yards — to boost Tech to a 36-10 lead.

Andre Davis' recovery of an Andre Kendrick fumble in the Miami end zone wrapped up the scoring.

• *Tech coach Frank Beamer questions an official's call.*

Miami	10	0	0	0	—	10
Virginia Tech	7	7	6	23	—	43

• *Hokie defenders Derek Carter and Philip Hicks wrap up Miami halfback Clinton Portis (28).*

Tech Completes Perfect Season in Rout of BC

BLACKSBURG, Nov. 26, 1999 — Michael Vick, the Hokies' master magician, ran and passed for 366 yards and threw for three touchdowns to lead No. 2-ranked Virginia Tech past the No. 22 Boston College Eagles, 38-14.

The win gave the Hokies their greatest season in 106 years of playing college football, a third Big East title and a national championship showdown with No. 1 Florida State in the Sugar Bowl on Jan. 4, 2000.

Andre Davis gained 172 yards on five receptions and scored twice for the Hokies (11-0, 7-0 in the Big East) to lead the Hokies, who clinched their first undefeated season since 1954.

The Eagles (8-3, 4-3 in the Big East) fell short of pulling off the upset but are still likely to land a bowl berth.

Vick finished the day 11 of 13 passing for 291 yards, and also ran for 76 yards and added a rushing touchdown on 16 carries in the victory.

Shyrone Stith, Tech's workhorse all season, cracked the goal line from three yards out just 2:36 into the contest to put Tech ahead, 7-0. Stith finished with 97 yards on 23 carries to lead the Hokies' ground game.

Tech took a 14-point edge early in the second quarter when Vick hooked up with Davis for a 69-yard touchdown strike. The duo connected again

four minutes later, this time a 59-yard score, to make it 21-0 with 9:12 left until the break.

Shayne Graham added a 40-yard field goal with 2:40 to play until the intermission to give the Hokies a 24-0 lead. In addition to increasing his team's lead, Graham's field goal made him the new Big East single-season scoring leader with 105 points.

Virginia Tech continued to move the ball in the second half, but were denied on fourth-and-goal from the BC 1-yard line with two minutes remaining in the third quarter.

Inspired by the defensive stand, Boston College got into the end zone just two plays later. Dedrick Dewalt caught a Tim Hasselbeck pass at the 40-yard line and took it the distance, 97 yards, for a touchdown to make it 24-7 with 1:08 remaining in the third quarter.

Hasselbeck was 6 for 19 passing for 138 yards and one touchdown in a losing cause, while Dewalt led the Eagles with 97 yards receiving.

But Vick and the Hokies answered on their next possession as the freshman signal caller finished an impressive drive with a 29-yard touchdown pass to Cullen Hawkins. Vick's third touchdown pass of the day made it 31-7 with 12:37 still to play in the fourth quarter.

Vick wrapped up Tech's scoring with a four-yard touchdown scramble with 3:27 left in the game. The speedy southpaw took the snap and went untouched

*Frank Beamer enjoys a victory ride after
Tech completed an 11-0 regular season.*

• **Top: Tech fans wore their pride for the BC game. Right: Nick Sorenson (14) kept BC quarterback Tim Hasselbeck on the run all afternoon.**

around left end to make it 38-7.

But Boston College still had some fight left and added another touchdown in the waning minutes. William Green took a handoff on a draw play and rambled 45 yards down the left sideline to make it 38-14 with less than one minute remaining.

Boston College	**0**	**0**	**7**	**7** —	**14**
Virginia Tech	**7**	**17**	**0**	**14** —	**38**

Seminoles Survive Hokies' Comeback to Win Title Game

NEW ORLEANS, Jan. 4, 2000 - Florida State, who was No. 1 at the start of the season and No. 1 at the finish, is the perfect national champion.

Led by the sizzling receiver Peter Warrick and steady quarterback Chris Weinke, the Seminoles held off Virginia Tech for a 46-29 win tonight in the Sugar Bowl.

The Hokies' freshman quarterback, Michael Vick, played an electrifying game of catch-me-if you-can, but it wasn't enough.

Warrick thrilled a sellout Superdome crowd with a record 20-point game — he caught touchdown passes of 64 and 43 yards, returned a punt 59 yards for a touchdown and snagged a 2-point pass from Weinke.

The 27-year-old Weinke completed 20 of 34 passes for 329 yards and four TD's — two to Warrick and two to Ron Dugans. Warrick finished with six catches for 163 yards in the highest-scoring Sugar Bowl in history.

Vick threw for 225 yards and one TD ran for 97 yards and another touchdown.

Florida State (12-0) was certain to become the first team to go wire-to-wire in The Associated Press' poll since the preseason ratings began in 1950. The final AP poll will be released early today to confirm the obvious.

The Seminoles were automatically crowned national champs in the USA Today-ESPN coaches' poll under the Bowl Championship Series format.

All week, Warrick and his senior pals promised each other they would do everything possible to avoid losing three title games. They did — in a big way — and Bobby Bowden completed a remarkable year. He won his 300th game in the first father vs. son coaching matchup, celebrated his 70th birthday and 50th wedding anniversary and finally attained his first perfect season in 40 years as a coach.

Warrick, the all-American wide receiver who lost his chance at the Heisman Trophy after a two-game suspension for his role in a shopping mall scam, came up with his best performance in the final game of his college career.

In the first half, he caught three passes for 100 yards and his punt return helped the Seminoles build a 28-14 lead after 30 minutes of big plays. Lasst season, he was held to one catch for 7 yards in a Fiesta Bowl loss to Tennessee in the national title game. In fact, in three previous bowl games, Warrick totaled five catches and no TD's.

He opened the scoring with his 64-yard grab, then took a punt and blazed past Tech defenders for a 59-yard TD and a 28-7 lead.

Late in the game, with half of the crowd of 79,280 chanting "Peter Warrick, Peter Warrick," Weinke reared back and threw a 43-yard TD pass to the Warrick, who caught the ball while diving into the

Peter Warrick (9), who caught six passes for 163 yards and 2 TD's, snags a pass from Tech defensive back Anthony Midget.

end zone with a Virginia Tech defender draped over him.

The win over the upstart Hokies (11-1) stamped the Seminoles as the team of the Decade.

The loss ended Virginia Tech's dream season to and a bid for its first national title in 107 years of playing football.

Vick was valiant in defeat. The 19-year-old left-hander overcame a lost fumble near the Seminoles' goal line on the game-opening drive and led the Hokies back from a 21-point deficit to a 29-28 lead with 2:13 left in the third quarter.

Florida State somehow regrouped and regained the lead as Weinke hit Dugans on a 15-yard TD pass with 12:59 left in the game. Warrick caught a 2-point pass from Weinke to put FSU back in the lead, 36-29.

Florida State got the ball back when linebacker Bobby Rhodes' helmet knocked the ball from Vick's grasp and safety Sean Key recovered at the Hokies' 34. The turnover set up Sebastian Janikowski's 32-yard field goal with 10:26 that put the Seminoles ahead, 39-29.

And then came Warrick's best catch of all to seal the title. After stopping Tech on fourth Tech on fourth down, FSU took over at the Tech 43 and Weinke found Warrick, who held onto the ball with corner-back Roynell Whitaker hanging over him.

Down 28-14 at the half, Virginia Tech seized the momentum. Vick threw a 26-yard completion to set up Shayne Graham's 23-yard field goal to narrow the score to 28-17.

The Hokies' defense came alive and forced a punt, which was returned 46 yards to the Seminoles' 36 by Ike Carlton, the cornerback subbing for injured Ricky Hall.

Three plays later, Andre Kendrick raced 29 yards for a touchdown to pull the Hokies to within 29-23. Kendrick had stepped in for Shyrone Smith, Tech's 1,000-yard rusher who missed the second half with a sprained ankle. Vick's 2-point pass fell incomplete.

Michael Vick (7) ran for 97 yards and 1 TD and passed for 225 yards and a touchdown.

Virginia Tech	7	7	15	0	—	29
Florida State	14	14	0	18	—	46

Frank Beamer: He Took The Hokies to the Top

When Frank Beamer first arrived at Virginia Tech in 1965, he was an All-South quarterback from Hillsville, Va.

After one day of practice, the 5-9 signal caller became a defensive back. He would go on to become a three-year starter for the Hokies.

Tech would post a record of 22-9-1 during this three-year period and played in the Liberty Bowl twice — in 1966 against Miami and again in 1968 against Ole Miss.

It was one of the Hokies' finest hours.

After graduation, Beamer would enter coaching. He began as an assistant at Radford High, working for Harold Absher. The Bobcats won the state title in 1971. Beamer later became a graduate assistant at Maryland in 1972 after his old coach, Jerry Claiborne, had taken over.

He would later join Bobby Ross' staff at The Citadel and Mike Gottfried's staff at Murray State, where he became noted as a defensive coach.

When Gottfried left to become head coach at Cincinnati in 1980, Beamer was tapped to succeed him. In six seasons with the Racers, Beamer led them to a 42-23-2 record and an Ohio Valley Conference title in 1986.

After the 1986 season, Beamer was asked to return to his alma mater to replace Bill Dooley, who had resigned following the 1986 Peach Bowl.

It would take Beamer nearly seven seasons to build Tech into a big-time winner, but since 1993 Tech has averaged more than 9 wins per season — a total unmatched by any previous Hokie coach.

Beamer's Hokies have now won two Big East titles outright — in 1995 and 1999, and a share of the 1996 Big East championship. He has also led Tech to the Sugar Bowl twice (in 1995 and 2000) and the 1996 Orange Bowl.

In 1999, Tech spent the second half of the season ranked No. 2 in the country and played Florida State in the Sugar Bowl for the national championship.

The Beamer File

	W	L	T
1987	2	9	0
1988	3	8	0
1989	6	4	1
1990	6	5	0
1991	5	6	0
1992	2	8	1
1993	9	3	0
1994	8	4	0
1995	10	2	0
1996	10	2	0
1997	7	5	0
1998	9	3	0
1999	11	1	0
Total	88	60	2

• *Frank Beamer starred as a defensive back at Tech from 1966-68. He later returned as the Hokies' head coach in 1987 and has led Virginia Tech to its greatest era of college football.*

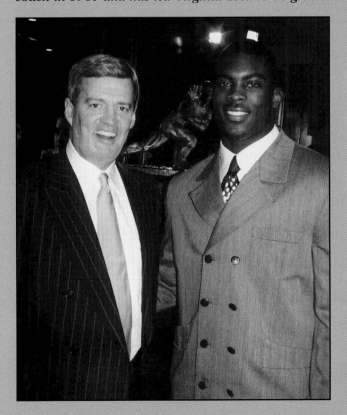

AP/Wide World: 123, 124, 125, 127, 128, 129, 131, 132, 133, 136.

Allsport Photography USA: 139, 140-141, Backcover.

Frank Beamer Family: 143-all.

Virginia Tech Special Collections: Front Cover, 18, 20, 21-both, 22, 23-both, 25-both, 27-all, 29-top, 31-both, 35-both, 37, 39, 53.

Virginia Tech Sports Information: 29-bottom, 33-all, 41, 43, 44, 45-all, 46-47, 49, 51, 54-55, 56, 57, 59, 61, 63, 65, 67, 69, 71, 73, 74-75, 76, 77, 79, 80-both, 81-both, 83, 85, 86, 88-89, 91, 92-93, 95, 96-both, 97, 99, 100-101, 103, 104, 104-105, 107, 108-109, 109,111, 112, 112-113, 115, 116-both, 117, 119, 120, 121-both, 135, 136-137.